AFRICAN AMERICAN
WOMEN WRITERS

◆

BLACK ✦ STARS

AFRICAN AMERICAN WOMEN WRITERS

✦

BRENDA WILKINSON

JIM HASKINS, GENERAL EDITOR

John Wiley & Sons, Inc.

New York • Chichester • Weinheim • Brisbane • Singapore • Toronto

Published by John Wiley & Sons, Inc.
Published simultaneously in Canada

Design and composition by Navta Associates, Inc.

This publication is designed to provide accurate and authoritative information in regard
to the subject matter covered. It is sold with the understanding that the publisher is
not engaged in rendering professional services. If professional advice or other expert
assistance is required, the services of a competent professional person should be sought.

Library of Congress Cataloging-in-Publication Data

Wilkinson, Brenda
        African American women writers / Brenda Wilkinson.
            p.   cm. — (Black star series)
        Includes bibliographical references and index.
        Summary: Discusses the lives and work of such notable African
American women authors as: Phillis Wheatley, Ida B. Wells-Barnett,
Zora Neale Hurston, Gwendolyn Brooks, Nikki Giovanni, and Terry
McMillan.
        ISBN 0-471-17580-3 (alk. paper)
        1. American literature—Afro-American authors—History and
criticism Juvenile literature.   2. American literature—Women
authors—History and criticism Juvenile literature.   3. Afro-
American women authors Biography Juvenile literature.
[1. Authors, American.   2. Afro-Americans Biography   3. Women
Biography.   4. American literature—Afro-American authors—History
and criticism.]   I. Title.   II. Series: Black stars (New York, N.Y.)
PS153.N5W49   2000
810.9'9287—DC21   99-25552

Printed in the United States of America
10   9   8   7   6   5   4   3   2

In memory of beloved mothers:
Ethel Anderson Scott and Anna Jamerson Thompson

CONTENTS

ACKNOWLEDGMENTS

I wish to acknowledge the many women writers of scholarly nonfiction, whose anthologies, biographies, and essays served as sources of information in my research for this book for young readers.

INTRODUCTION
"DICK, JANE, AND ME"

✦

As a young black girl growing up in the segregated South of the 1950s, I was not allowed to use the public library. The only reading material I had during these years was provided by my elementary and Sunday school teachers. I truly loved books, and remember caressing the first ones my older sister brought home from school. I have clear memories at age four of running up the street to meet my sister as she came home from school each day, and begging her to let me carry her books. I would then walk proudly up the street pretending that I too was a schoolgirl who could read!

In first grade, I was introduced to the *Dick and Jane* series, which were the standard books used in classrooms across the country to teach children how to read. The main characters were Dick, Jane, Mother, Father, their dog Spot, and Puff, their cat. Dick and Jane's family and all their neighbors were white. They spoke in short, choppy sentences:

"Look, Jane!
See Spot.
See Spot jump and play."

Although we did learn to read through this series of books, there was nothing in these stories to spark a child's imagination—and for children of color, nothing with which we could identify. Having no material to reflect and affirm who we were as people of color resulted in low self-esteem for many black children like me.

Not only were all the characters in our school textbooks white, but so were nearly all the people in commercial advertisements. There were a few exceptions like Uncle Ben on a rice box, Aunt Jemima on pancake mix, and exaggerated, cartoon-type figures on various detergent products. All mass-market toy figures for children were white, as were all the characters in comic books and on most American television programs.

It is no wonder that when I began drawing as an adolescent, my first sketches of people were girls with yellow hair. My main model was Little Miss Sunbeam, a blond girl who appeared on the wrappers of white bread and in advertisements on the screen doors of nearly every country store across the South during the 1950s.

Although my family, friends, and everyone around me had brown skin and black hair, my mind's eye captured the public images. While I clearly loved my family and the people in my community, the fact that no one else depicted them suggested that I too should only draw what was white.

Betty, a blond character in the *Archie* comic book series, became my second model. There was a dark-haired girl, Veronica, in the same series, but so captivated was I by the golden-haired girl of white bread, that I continued to color hair yellow.

This inability to love ourselves was not exclusive to children; some grown-ups experienced it as well. I recall one Christmas when a foolish woman relative, upon seeing the first Negro doll that my parents purchased for me and my sisters, picked it up and stated that she would never buy anything "so ugly" for her children. So not only

were the young misguided, but so were many adults. It would take a political movement to change this situation.

The civil rights movement brought significant social change. Black people began to search for greater understanding of their beginnings in this country—and in looking back, discovered much to take pride in as a race of people. We discovered the rich legacy from which we came and began to view ourselves differently. We looked with new eyes at our complexions, the texture of our hair, our facial features, and more. While a Negro child of my generation could be punished for uttering the word *black* in reference to a sibling or peer, by the late 1960s it was the preferred term that most African Americans used.

Suddenly we were worshiping our dark selves. Celebrating how we looked and all we had accomplished brought a renewed interest in Africa, the place of our origin. We adopted African models of living and popularized African names, hairstyles, clothing, and jewelry. But this new thinking was a gradual process. It was not easy to cast aside all the negative images deeply embedded in our minds about blackness, some of which sadly remain today among both blacks and whites.

Literature played a major role in our changing attitudes. Recognizing the need for people of color to have images that affirm them and experiences to identify with, librarians and publishers began seeking more materials about ethnic minorities. It was during this period that I, and many other African Americans as well as Hispanic Americans and Asian Americans who had studied and were pursuing writing careers, had an opportunity to enter the publishing world. Some became editors; others received contracts to write fiction, non-fiction, and poetry. Young adult books (the area I chose) and books for younger children that told the stories of people of color were in great demand by publishers. Libraries purchased and displayed these new books prominently.

This was a time of glory for me. I read everything I could get my hands on and practically *lived* at the library! All these experiences resulted in the writing and publication of my first book, *Ludell*, a coming-of-age novel of a young girl in the South during the 1950s. Since *Ludell*, I have written several books for young adults, the last of which is a history of the civil rights movement. Much of the research for that book helped prepare me for this history of African American women writers.

I have been keenly interested in the work of black women writers and have read numerous books by and about them over the past twenty-five years. I treasure the stories they tell and am touched by the sacrifices they made to tell these stories. Most of these writers have persevered against tremendous odds, and although black women are being published in greater numbers today, it is important to acknowledge that this has not always been the case.

It is important to note that this is not a book of every black woman who ever lifted a pen, but a collection of biographies of significant women writers with whom you will want to become familiar throughout your teenage years. You may consider this as a collection of black women authors you should know something about by the time you graduate from high school.

As you continue to learn about these various writers, you may discover that some of these books are too complex for teenage readers. Just remember that you don't need to rush to read every book written by Toni Morrison or Alice Walker; beginning to know who these women are and their contributions to American literature is the important thing. You may choose to read some of their writings in junior high, while others may be more appropriate in high school, and others in college and beyond. (See also pages 144–146 for a list of African American writers for children.)

As you learn who these black women writers are, you will come to

understand the importance of seeking out their works. The stories they tell and the experiences they share can

- ✦ improve your analytical skills,
- ✦ give you the confidence to solve particular problems,
- ✦ offer you the comfort and reassurance that you are not the first to experience difficulty,
- ✦ give you a greater understanding of the world,
- ✦ illustrate that greatness can be achieved at all social and economic levels,
- ✦ entertain you.

And I know these women's life stories will help you grow more gracefully into adulthood.

✦

THE
EARLY YEARS

PHILLIS
WHEATLEY

(1753?–1784)

In the summer of 1761, a ship named the *Phillis* arrived in Boston. A small and fragile girl, no more than eight years old, stood shivering at the dock. Sickness and fear consumed her trembling body, which she attempted to cover with an old piece of carpet.

Kidnapped from Africa and sold into slavery, Phillis was named for the slave ship on which she was brought to America. Her birthplace is unknown, but research has placed the point of her capture on the west coast of Africa, the present-day nations of Senegal and Gambia. How frightening it must have been for Phillis—first, to be torn away from her family and village, and then to endure the cruel voyage.

This young girl was destined to become one of America's brightest stars. A future poet and author of the first collection of poetry by an African American, she was at that moment a piece of property awaiting the highest bidder. Along with approximately seventy-five other Africans, she was part of the human cargo of Captain Peter Gwinn, who worked for Timothy Fitch, slave merchant and owner of the *Phillis*.

PHILLIS WHEATLEY NEGRO SERVANT to Mr JOHN WHEATLEY, of BOSTON.

10

Along with the small number of survivors, young Phillis had been splashed with a bucket of water and was presented for sale at the Boston docks. Among the speculators at the Boston slave auction was Susannah Wheatley, wife of John Wheatley, a wealthy Boston tailor. The mother of eighteen-year-old twins, Mary and Nathaniel Wheatley, Susannah was in search of a young servant of "healthy" appearance. Something about the trembling and half-naked girl captured her attention. Perhaps it was Susannah's own poor health, or that of her fragile daughter, Mary, that evoked such pity and made her choose the sickly girl.

Phillis Wheatley's tribal and religious African roots are not known. But based on Phillis's point of capture and on her own early recollections, some historians believe that she was a member of the Fulani, a Muslim tribe of western Africa. As a girl, she shared a story of a faint memory of her mother kneeling before the sunrise, a Muslim ritual.

Whatever religious grounding young Phillis may have had, it was displaced by the influence of Christianity, the religion of her owners, whose customs she accepted as her own.

Phillis quickly adjusted to life in the Wheatley household, where she would remain for seventeen years. The Wheatleys recognized the

AFRICANS IN COLONIAL TIMES

When Phillis arrived in America, 230,000 blacks lived in the colonies. Some 16,000, like Phillis, were enslaved in New England, where they worked primarily as servants and were allowed to learn to read and write. But most were enslaved in the South, where they labored on rice, cotton, and tobacco plantations. Southern "slave codes" denied blacks many privileges: learning to read or write, defending themselves against abuse by whites, testifying against whites in court, and owning property.

young slave girl's hunger for knowledge and encouraged her. Eighteen-year-old Mary Wheatley, who was sickly like Phillis, became a constant companion. The two spent extended periods of time reading the Bible and studying poetry. Phillis Wheatley soon learned to read English, and by age nine was studying Latin and the Bible.

At age twelve, she began to write poetry. The Wheatleys provided paper, pen, and ink and allowed her to burn a candle until late into the night. Because of her poor health, Phillis was virtually cut off from other African Americans, so she found companionship in words. The Wheatleys treated Phillis differently from their other slaves. They assigned her light household duties, such as the dusting and polishing of furniture or the arranging of tables for dinner parties. They even scolded Prince, their driver, for keeping Phillis up front beside him in the cold, damp weather, instead of letting her sit inside their carriage.

The one close relationship that Phillis was able to develop with another slave was with Obour Tanner. They met in Rhode Island, where their owners spent their vacation. Like Phillis, Tanner was educated by her owners and was a devout Christian. The two young women established a long friendship through their letters.

Phillis Wheatley started to gain recognition in 1770 with the publication of a verse she wrote in 1767 in memory of the Reverend George Whitefield, a famed Methodist evangelist. In 1768, she wrote a patriotic verse, "On the Arrival of the Ships of War, and Landing of the Troops," in response to the arrival in Boston of British troops sent to quell colonial unrest.

Phillis became a source of great pride to the Wheatley family, and they began to invite prominent Bostonians to meet and hear her. Among those invited was Eunice Fitch, wife of the merchant upon whose slave ship Phillis had arrived in America. Governor Thomas Hutchins and legislator John Hancock gave the aspiring young artist books to encourage her.

In 1773, Nathaniel Wheatley had cause to travel to England on business. The family decided that Phillis Wheatley would accompany him on the trip. They had a special reason. American printers had refused to publish the writings of a slave girl, so Nathaniel Wheatley took Phillis to London to publish her book. She gave it the title *Poems on Various Subjects, Religious and Moral, by Phillis Wheatley, Negro Servant to Mrs. Wheatley of Boston.*

✦An author's work is **published** when it has been printed and distributed to the public.

✦A **protégé** (*protégée* when referring to a woman) is someone who is protected and/or trained by a person of greater experience or influence.

Her visit to London was glorious. To Phillis's surprise, word of her accomplishment as a poet had reached England before her arrival. London society embraced her. She became a protégée of both Lady Huntingdon and Lord Darmouth, who was then mayor of London. Other dignitaries who welcomed and encouraged her included Benjamin Franklin, who later became a prominent political figure in America, and Brooke Watson, who would become the mayor of London.

Unfortunately, Susannah Wheatley became severely ill, and Phillis's stay in London came to an end. She left London a few weeks short of the publication of her book. She was approximately twenty years old when she returned to Boston in September 1773. It would prove an eventful month for Phillis Wheatley. She was emancipated by John Wheatley and her book was released.

Some individuals who believed that people of African heritage were incapable of "thinking," let alone "writing," questioned that Phillis was the genuine author of the book. So her mistress, Susannah Wheatley, needed to prove that Phillis was indeed the true author. Thus, a certificate signed by prominent white men of New England was printed in the book. It read in part: "We whose names are under-written, do assure the world that the poems specified in the following pages were (as verily we believe) written by Phillis,

a young Negro girl." Susannah Wheatley died shortly afterward.

Phillis Wheatley continued to write poetry right up to the beginning of the American Revolution. She wrote to and was acknowledged by General George Washington in 1775. The general invited her to visit his headquarters, which she did the following year. Altogether, Phillis would publish five books of poetry and letters.

Following the death of John Wheatley in 1778, Phillis, who had remained part of the Wheatley household, was now on her own. That same year she married John Peters. Stories about her husband vary. Some say that John Peters held a variety of jobs—lawyer, grocer, banker, and doctor— but that he was unsuccessful in all of these occupations. Others labeled him a ne'er-do-well who shunned hard labor. It is difficult, however, to determine Peters's true character given the prejudice of the day. Whatever the true story, serious financial problems landed him in debtor's jail in 1784.

Phillis gave birth to three children, two of whom died as infants. Her third child died in 1784. Phillis died soon after on December 7, 1784, destitute and living in a boardinghouse in Boston. Announcement of her funeral was placed in two local papers: "Last Lord's Day, died Mrs. Phillis Peters (formerly Phillis Wheatley) aged 31, known to the world by her celebrated miscellaneous poems. Her funeral is to be this afternoon at four o'clock. . . . Her friends and acquaintances are desired to attend." Sadly, no one came.

Although Phillis Wheatley's five books were ignored for years after her death, and often dismissed as being too sentimental and patriotic, today her work is given the special honor it deserves. Indeed, a debt of gratitude is owed this early American poet for her discipline and determination. With the site of her grave unknown, the city of Boston honored her some two hundred years after her death by erecting a monument in her name.

A POET SHARES HER FEELINGS

"In every human breast, God has implanted a principle, which we call love of freedom; it is impatient of oppression and pants for deliverance. I will assert that same principle lives in us."

—Phillis Wheatley

SOJOURNER
TRUTH

(1797–1883)

✦

Unlike Phillis Wheatley, most slaves faced endless days of labor and harsh treatment. Slaves who dared show defiance were subjected to severe beatings and other savage acts of punishment. Many blacks risked all by running away. Among those who ran was the bold and brave woman who came to be known as Sojourner Truth.

Sojourner Truth was born in Ulster County, New York, in 1797. Her named was Isabella, and she was owned by a Dutchman named Ardinburgh. During her youth, she was separated from her parents and passed through a succession of cruel masters, two of whom were named Baumfree and Hurley. Tall of stature and large of frame, she was exploited for her size and made to work excessively hard.

She watched her mother's grief as her siblings were sold away to other masters. Sojourner grew up to experience the same horror of giving birth to children, only to have them torn from her arms. It is not known how many children she had, but when she escaped in 1826, she took only an infant son with her.

Fleeing with her child in the middle of night, Sojourner crept through dangerous forests and swamps, terrified of being tracked by bloodhounds and bounty hunters. She knew what could happen if she were caught alive. Punishment for escapees ranged from beatings after which a solution of salt and vinegar was poured on open wounds, to the cutting off of body parts, such as toes and fingers. Sojourner clutched her infant tightly. A baby could not understand the need to be silent in face of miseries that may have included unbearable heat or cold, bites of various insects, and insufficient food and water.

As Sojourner and other slaves stole their way through the nights, sympathizers—both black and white—risked their own safety, giving shelter, food, and water along the way. As a fugitive slave, she made her way safely to New York and was emancipated the following year, 1827.

In 1843, while working as a maid in New York City, Sojourner became convinced that she had been called to go out into the world and "travel about the land spreading truth to the people." Changing her name to Sojourner Truth, she became a preacher. Sojourner testified. Describing the suffering she had lived through, she soon became a major spokesperson for the abolitionist movement. Along with Frederick Douglass and William Lloyd Garrison, she became a significant leader in the struggle for emancipation.

Some people mocked her and spread rumors that she was a man disguised in women's garments. To dispel these rumors, she once publicly revealed her breast, then told the stunned audience, "It is not my shame, but yours that I should do this."

Nothing could stop Sojourner Truth. One day as she attended a women's rights meeting in Akron, Ohio, clergymen argued that women should not have the right to vote. One dared to say that the fact that Christ was a man proved God considered women inferior to men. Sojourner rose to speak. Some of the suffragettes worried that a former slave was not a proper spokesperson for them and would only

bring ridicule to their cause. They gestured for her to return to her seat. But the president of the group, Frances Dana Gage, ignored them and welcomed Sojourner to the podium.

"Ain't I a Woman?," the courageous speech Sojourner gave that day, June 21, 1851, became etched in American history:

The acclaimed white author of the era, Harriet Beecher Stowe, wrote a special tribute to Sojourner in the *Atlantic Monthly*. In the 1863 article, Stowe said, "I do not recollect ever to have been conversant with any one who had more of that silent and subtle power which we call person presence than this woman."

During the Civil War, Sojourner Truth helped recruit soldiers and aided in relief efforts for freed men and women escaping from the South. As an adviser to President Abraham Lincoln, she used her influence to bring about the desegregation of streetcars in Washington, D.C.

Sojourner Truth never learned to read or write, but she often said, "I cannot read a book, but I can read the people." In 1850, with the

---

"AIN'T I A WOMAN?"

"That man over there says that women need to be helped into carriages and lifted over ditches, and to have the best help everywhere. Nobody ever helps me into carriages, or over mud-puddles, or gives me any best place. Well, I'm a woman, ain't I?

Look at my arms. I have ploughed, and planted, and gathered into barns, and no man could head me! And ain't I a woman?

I could work as much and eat as much as a man, when I could get it—and bear the lash as well. And ain't I a woman?

I have borne . . . children, and seen most all sold off to slavery, and when I cried out with a mother's grief, none but Jesus heard me! And ain't I a woman?"

—Sojourner Truth

One of Sojourner Truth's many roles was as an adviser to President Lincoln. They are shown here examining the Bible presented to them by people of Baltimore. Lincoln appointed her counselor to the Freedmen of Washington, a position she held until her retirement in 1875.

help of friends and family, she worked with Olive Gilbert to write and publish *Narrative of Sojourner Truth*; and she updated it with the assistance of Frances Titus. The expanded version, *Book of Life*, includes personal letters, newspaper stories of events in which she participated, and expressions of appreciation for her work sent to her from around the world. The narrative was reprinted in 1878, 1881, and 1884 with the title *Narrative of Sojourner Truth; A Bondswoman of Olden Time, With a History of Her Labors and Correspondence Drawn from Her "Book of Life."*

Sojourner Truth, one of America's greatest reformers, died at her home in Battle Creek, Michigan, in 1883.

TELL THAT STORY—THE ORAL TRADITION

Accounts of frightful journeys and all the horrors of slavery are known today largely because slaves passed these stories on through the "oral tradition" of storytelling. This became the means through which people without formal education helped preserve their histories and cultures until the day that someone else could write them down. Fortunately, Africans brought their oral traditions with them from their ancient cultures where storytelling was also important.

THE CIVIL WAR YEARS AND RECONSTRUCTION

HARRIET
JACOBS

(1813–1897)

◆

Born in Edenton, North Carolina, Harriet Jacobs was orphaned at an early age, a common situation for enslaved children. Eventually, she would also be separated from her brother, John. Harriet was never left totally alone, though. When her parents died, she was raised by her freed grandmother and a sympathetic mistress who taught her to read.

Harriet was barely eleven years old when her mistress died, and she was then turned over to an evil new master, Dr. James Norcom. She became the victim of his horrendous sexual abuse. She accepted the affection of another white man who helped protect her. With him, she gave birth to a son and a daughter. Still fearful, however, she fled alone, finding refuge in hiding at her grandmother's home. In a stroke of luck, the apparently abandoned children were given to Harriet's grandmother.

Harriet remained in her grandmother's home for seven years, hiding in a tiny attic. She passed the years reading the Bible, sewing,

and sneaking moments with her children. Through the help of friends, letters from her were directed to her owner from distant places; it did not occur to anyone to look for her at her grandmother's house.

Harriet Jacobs finally escaped and worked her way north. Reunited with her daughter, she found employment as a nursemaid to the infant child of editor, poet, and magazine writer Nathaniel Parker Willis. Jacobs wisely sought out anti-slavery activists in Rochester, New York, one of whom was her brother, John. Jacobs went to live with him, and together they operated an anti-slavery reading room and bookstore. It was located above the office where abolitionist and former slave Frederick Douglass published his newspaper, the *North Star*.

Through Jacobs's association with Douglass, she met Amy Post, an abolitionist and early feminist. It was Amy Post who, upon hearing

A WRITER'S COURAGE

Harriet Jacobs began writing her autobiography in the form of a novel, *Incidents in the Life of a Slave Girl* (1861). She published *Incidents* under the pseudonym of Linda Brent. She explained that there was no motive for secrecy on her own account—but that she felt the need to disguise important people and places because of the sensational nature of the story she wished to tell. She had no way to predict what the response to her book would be from either blacks or whites.

- ✦ A **novel** is a long work of prose fiction.
- ✦ A **pseudonym** is a made-up name or a pen name.
- ✦ When someone writes his or her own life story, it's called an **autobiography**.

Incidents describes the painful sexual exploitation of black girls and women under slavery. It took tremendous courage to tell such a sad and personal story— for although experienced by many, few could or would tell it. Some were too afraid, and some were too embarrassed. Most suffered in silence.

Jacobs's story, urged her to consider sharing it with others. Because of the widespread response to the publication of *Uncle Tom's Cabin*, the anti-slavery novel by Harriet Beecher Stowe, Jacobs solicited the support of the author, hoping that she would be interested in her story. No such support or interest, however, was forthcoming, but in 1861, Jacobs managed to get the book printed. With the Civil War occupying everyone's attention, Jacobs's story received little public attention except for that of abolitionist sympathizers.

From 1862 to 1866, Harriet Jacobs worked in Washington, D.C., with black Civil War refugees. After the war ended, she went to Savannah, Georgia, and continued to work in war relief efforts among

$200 Reward.

RANAWAY from the subscriber, on the night of Thursday, the 30th of Sepember,

FIVE NEGRO SLAVES,

To-wit : one Negro man, his wife, and three children.

The man is a black negro, full height, very erect, his face a little thin. He is about forty years of age, and calls himself *Washington Reed*, and is known by the name of Washington. He is probably well dressed, possibly takes with him an ivory headed cane, and is of good address. Several of his teeth are gone.

Mary, his wife, is about thirty years of age, a bright mulatto woman, and quite stout and strong.

The oldest of the children is a boy, of the name of FIELDING, twelve years of age, a dark mulatto, with heavy eyelids. He probably wore a new cloth cap.

MATILDA, the second child, is a girl, six years of age, rather a dark mulatto, but a bright and smart looking child.

MALCOLM, the youngest, is a boy, four years old, a lighter mulatto than the last, and about equally as bright. He probably also wore a cloth cap. If examined, he will be found to have a swelling at the navel.

Washington and Mary have lived at or near St. Louis, with the subscriber, for about 15 years.

It is supposed that they are making their way to Chicago, and that a white man accompanies them, that they will travel chiefly at night, and most probably in a covered wagon.

A reward of $150 will be paid for their apprehension, so that I can get them, if taken within one hundred miles of St. Louis, and $200 if taken beyond that, and secured so that I can get them, and other reasonable additional charges, if delivered to the subscriber, or to THOMAS ALLEN, Esq., at St. Louis, Mo. The above negroes, for the last few years, have been in possession of Thomas Allen, Esq., of St. Louis.

WM. RUSSELL.

ST. LOUIS, Oct. 1, 1847.

Owners advertised for the return of runaway slaves like Harriet Jacobs.

blacks. Upon returning to Washington, she became one of the founding organizers of the National Association of Colored Women. Harriet Jacobs remained in Washington until her death on March 7, 1897.

INCIDENTS IN THE LIFE OF A SLAVE GIRL

"I have not written my experiences in order to attract attention to myself; on the contrary, it would have been more pleasant to me to have been silent about my own history. Neither do I care to excite sympathy for my own sufferings. But I do earnestly desire to arouse the women of the North to a realizing sense of the condition of two millions of women at the South, still in bondage, suffering what I suffered, and most of them far worse. I want to add my testimony to that of abler pens to convince the people of the Free States what Slavery really is. Only by experience can any one realize how deep, and dark, and foul is that pit of abominations."

—Harriet Jacobs

FRANCES E. W.
HARPER

(1825–1911)

✦

Frances Ellen Watkins Harper's novel *Iola Leroy* (1892) was the best-selling novel by an African American in the nineteenth century. It is the saga of educated, light-skinned, free blacks who are sold into slavery. Iola and her brother join the Union army as a nurse and a soldier, respectively, and then reunite, older and much wiser, after the long Civil War.

Born on September 24, 1825, in Baltimore, Maryland, Frances Ellen Watkins was the spirited only child of free parents. Orphaned by age three, she was raised by an aunt and uncle. Frances's uncle was a minister, writer, and educator who made sure that his niece read the Bible and practiced writing every day. At age thirteen, Frances was hired out to do domestic work, but she continued to study during her leisure time.

Frances loved words and in 1845 published a book of poetry titled *Forest Leaves*. Unfortunately, no copy of the book remains today. She continued to write and eventually produced four novels and numerous volumes of poetry, short stories, and essays during her long,

31

rewarding life. Frances's first career was as a teacher. Hired as the first female teacher at Union Seminary, a school organized by the African Methodist Episcopal Church, she later taught in Little York, Pennsylvania.

Because of the Fugitive Slave Laws, Frances Watkins and all free blacks traveling around the country risked being seized in any slave-holding state and declared a slave. Living with such restrictions frustrated her. And more than this, it troubled her to read news stories of those who suffered daily with slave codes and worse. Frances decided to resign from her teaching position in the 1850s and dedicate all her time to fighting slavery.

Writing became Frances's weapon. "Eliza Harris," written in response to Harriet Beecher Stowe's 1853 publication of *Uncle Tom's Cabin*, brought praise from abolitionists Frederick Douglass and William Lloyd Garrison. Both men began reserving space for her protests in their publications. They also wrote complimentary introductions to some of her writings. Frances was hired as a speaker by the Maine Anti-Slavery Society, which led to other speaking invitations from other abolitionist groups.

The author's publication of *Poems on Miscellaneous Subjects* in 1854 (which featured an introduction by William Lloyd Garrison) sold more than 10,000 copies in its first printing. Reprinted more than twenty times during her lifetime, it also became a favorite among young militant poets of the 1960s because of its fiery tone. Many young blacks were inspired to write protest poetry against segregation after discovering Frances Watkins's protest poems and essays.

As emancipation seemed further out of reach than ever, Frances Watkins grew more militant. When abolitionist John Brown failed in his attempt to start a slave rebellion at Harpers Ferry, Virginia (now West Virginia), in 1859, Frances led a campaign of support for him. There was no chance of securing the freedom of John Brown, his sons, or the black men who took part in the failed raid. But Frances felt she

could at least write to the families of the men who awaited the gallows. She also helped raise financial support for the families. As Watkins wrote in a newspaper editorial, "It is not enough to express our sympathy by words. We should be ready to crystallize it into action."

In 1860, the author married Fenton Harper, a widower with three children. They lived on his farm in Columbus, Ohio, where Frances gave birth to a daughter. Fenton Harper died four years after their marriage. With debts absorbing most of her husband's assets, Frances Harper returned to the lecture circuit. She also became one of the many teachers who traveled south after the Civil War to teach newly freed slaves.

In her collection *Sketches of Southern Life* (1872), Harper creates a sixty-year-old ex-slave, Aunt Chloe, a witty character who tells the story of slavery and Reconstruction—and how she triumphs in the end. The conversational style that Harper used to tell these stories would be used by future writers such as the famous poet Langston Hughes. In her Philadelphia newspaper column, Harper used the same technique, imaginary conversations, this time between a female college graduate and her aunt, to comment on the ideas of the day. Above all, Harper wanted "to awaken the hearts" of Americans to injustice, religion, and morality.

◆ A **character** is any person in a story.

◆ Each writer develops her own style or **technique** for telling a story.

Frances Harper was co-founder and officer of the National Association of Colored Women and she also served with the National Council of Women, the Universal Peace Union, the Women's Christian Temperance Union, and other clubs and organizations. The author died of heart disease on February 20, 1911, and was eulogized at the Unitarian Church in Eden Cemetery, Philadelphia.

A Protest Poem

The Slave Auction

The sale began—young girls were there,
Defenseless in their wretchedness,
Whose stifled sobs of deep despair
Revealed their anguish and distress.

And mothers stood with streaming eyes,
And saw their dearest children sold;
Unheeded rose their bitter cries,
While tyrants bartered them for gold.

—Frances E. W. Harper

IDA B.
WELLS-BARNETT

(1862–1931)

The Civil War in no way ended injustice toward African Americans. Blacks needed people to speak out and speak up for their new rights. One of the most courageous voices was that of Ida B. Wells-Barnett, a crusading journalist and early feminist.

Ida, the eldest of Lizzie Bell and James Wells's eight children, was born in Holly Springs, Mississippi, just six months before President Lincoln issued the Emancipation Proclamation freeing all slaves in the Confederacy. Her parents rejoiced in her freedom. James Wells became a leader in the Freedmen's Bureau, an organization established by the government in 1865 to help former slaves rebuild their lives. He and Lizzie Bell also helped set up a school for black children. Northern church missionaries, many of whom made great sacrifices entering the hostile atmosphere of the South, came to help. Ida was one of their first students.

All these positive experiences made Ida feel strong and confident. So she was prepared when tragedy struck. At age sixteen, Ida's childhood ended abruptly. Both her parents and her youngest brother died

36

of a yellow fever epidemic in 1878. Ida became responsible for her siblings. After graduating from Rust, a high school and industrial school in Holly Springs Mississippi, and passing the teacher's exam, she began a career as a teacher, earning $25 per month. She later moved to Memphis for a higher-paid position.

Wells somehow found time to attend classes at Fisk, a historically black college, which led to another big change in her life. She discovered journalism. She wrote for the student newspaper. She also became editor of the *Evening Star* and the *Living Way*, two black church publications. The more jobs she had, the more money she could send home to her family.

✦ An **editor** helps authors prepare their work for publication.

✦ When a work is **edited**, it is usually checked for accuracy and clarity.

Using the pen name Iola (from her friend Frances Harper's novel), Wells often wrote about race. She frequently got her subject matter from her own personal experiences. For example, she refused to sit in the Jim Crow car on a train in the South. She sued the railroad company and won, but her case was later overturned by a Tennessee state court. She wrote about the railroad lawsuit in the church publications. She also wrote about the inequality between the public education of black children and that of white children in the South. By 1891, local

A WRITER DISCOVERS HER STYLE

Ida B. Wells's writing was very plain and direct. On her decision to write this way, she said, "I had an instinctive feeling that the people who had little or no school training should have something coming into their homes weekly which dealt with their problems in a simple, helpful way. So in weekly letters to the *Living Way*, I wrote in a plain, common-sense way on the things which concern our people."

white politicians learned that Wells was the writer behind these politically charged articles, and she was fired from her teaching position. Not to be silenced, Wells purchased part interest in a newspaper, the *Memphis Free Speech*. She became editor and eventually sole owner.

As African Americans struggled to establish their rightful place in America at the turn of the century, whites grew increasingly resentful. Mob violence became commonplace. Envy over blacks who attempted to build decent housing for themselves and anger over blacks competing for jobs and establishing businesses were only some of the resentments that exploded into senseless assaults on black lives. In March 1892, three black businessmen were lynched in Tennessee for attempting to establish a grocery store that competed with one owned by a white merchant. Local papers asserted that the cause of the lynching was an assault by Negro men on white women. The outraged and brave Ida B. Wells dared to write in response: "Nobody in this [black] section believes [that] old thread-bare lie."

Wells asserted instead that the lynchings were to discourage financial independence of blacks and the idea that white women could be interested in black men. These statements brought out a mob. Fortunately, she was away visiting Frances Harper at the time. Not only was the office of *Free Speech* destroyed, but Wells's partner, J. C. Fleming, was run out of town and Wells was warned not to return.

Establishing herself in New York, she continued her crusade against racial injustices in a newspaper, the *New York Age*, of which she later became editor and part owner. Publication of "A Red Record" (1895), one of many pamphlets she wrote, helped raise public awareness and action. The tone and writing style of "A Red Record" would be repeated years later in the speeches of civil rights advocates such as Dr. Martin Luther King Jr.

When blacks were barred from participation in the Chicago World's Fair, Wells joined Frederick Douglass and others in leading a protest campaign. She also began a campaign to have the word *Negro*

capitalized in the press, pointing out that French, German, Dutch, and Japanese were always capitalized.

In 1895, she married Ferdinan Barnett, a Chicago lawyer and editor of the *Chicago Conservator*. The couple became partners in social action. Ida B. Wells-Barnett is reported to have crusaded with all four of her children when they were infants, nursing them along the way. A founding member of the National Association for the Advancement of Colored People, in 1898 she presented to President William McKinley resolutions drafted against lynching. She organized one of the first African American suffrage groups, and in 1930, co-founded the National Association of Colored Women and the National Afro-American Council. She also ran as an independent candidate for Illinois state senator. By the time of her death in Chicago on March 25, 1931, she was known nationally and internationally. Her autobiography, *Crusade for Justice*, edited by her daughter, Alfreda M. Duster, was published in 1970.

INTO THE NEW CENTURY

JESSIE REDMON
FAUSET

(1884–1961)

✦

While African American writers were telling their stories, white authors were also writing versions of black life, many of which were inaccurate. Jessie Redmon Fauset didn't like being misrepresented. She wanted to show a different point of view.

One of the most prolific and scholarly writers of her generation, Fauset was strongly committed to her race. Rather than remain angry and preoccupied with someone else's distortions, she chose to tell her own truths. She became a major influence in the Harlem Renaissance, the flowering of black literature in the 1920s.

Born in Camden, New Jersey, in 1884, Jessie Redmon Fauset grew up in Philadelphia in a poor but stable and dignified family. The seventh child of the Reverend Redmon and Anna Seamon Fauset, she excelled in school. In 1905, Fauset became the first black woman to graduate from Cornell University and the first black woman to be admitted to Phi Beta Kappa, the top national honor society.

Despite her outstanding qualifications, she could not find work in Philadelphia because of racial discrimination. She finally secured a

44

teaching job in Baltimore, and later taught at Dunbar High School in Washington, D.C. Dunbar High would become famous because of superb educators like Jessie Fauset. Many black scholars were on the faculty. Fauset taught Latin and French at Dunbar for fourteen years.

To advance her studies, Jessie Fauset traveled to Paris, France, where she earned a master's degree in French from the Sorbonne, a prestigious university. After she returned to the United States, she began to submit fiction and poetry to *Crisis* magazine, the publication of the National Association for the Advancement of Colored People. Dr. W. E. B. Du Bois, who served as editor in chief, was so impressed with her writing that he asked her to come to New York and work for the magazine. His decision to hire her proved a wise one, since she went on to make a tremendous contribution, beginning as an editor in 1916 and serving in the position for seven years.

While working on *Crisis* in 1920, Jessie Fauset got a new assignment from Dr. Du Bois. He asked her to edit *The Brownies' Book*, a monthly magazine for children. Although the children's magazine remained in circulation for only two years, it touched the lives of thousands of black children. Jessie Fauset's contributions to the magazine were immeasurable. She not only edited submissions to *The Brownies' Book*, but wrote fiction, poetry, plays, songs, and translated foreign material. Many of the uncredited contributions to the magazine were by Jessie Fauset.

The Brownies' Book was not only a source of entertainment and education, it also shared news of world events. African American children of achievement across the country were also highlighted in this very special magazine. Finally, it served as a place where young people could send stories, write letters, and seek advice on personal problems.

Why did black children need a magazine of their own? Dr. Du Bois introduced *The Brownies' Book* with these words:

Heretofore the education of the Negro child has been too much in terms of white people. All through life his text-books contain much about white people and little or nothing about his own race. All the pictures he sees are of white people. Most of the books he reads are by white authors, and his heroes and heroines are white. If he goes to a moving picture show, the same is true. If a Negro appears on the screen, he is usually a caricature or a clown. The result is that all of the Negro child's idealism, all his sense of the good, the great and the beautiful is associated almost entirely with white people. The effect can be readily imagined. He unconsciously gets the impression that the Negro has little chance to be good, great, heroic or beautiful. . . .

In 1920, Jessie Fauset became the editor for the children's magazine The Brownies' Book. *She entertained and educated thousands of black children with the many stories, poems, plays, and songs she wrote for the magazine.*

Jessie Fauset's personal hope for black children was expressed in her dedication:

> To children, who with eager look
> scanned vainly library shelf and nook
> for History or Song or Story
> that told of Colored People's glory—
> we dedicate The Brownies' Book.

Along with the valuable contribution Jessie Fauset made to black children, she was mentor to some of the most famous black male writers of the era, including Langston Hughes, Countee Cullen, and Jean Toomer.

Fauset's other literary accomplishments include four adult novels: *There Is Confusion* (1924), *Plum Bun: A Novel Without a Moral* (1929), *The Chinaberry Tree* (1931), and *Comedy: American Style* (1933). *The Chinaberry Tree* was based on a true story that Fauset is reported to have heard at age fifteen.

Jessie Fauset felt the cruel sting of racial prejudice time and again. She was denied entry to the first college of her choice because she was black. She had difficulty landing a local teacher's job. And she could not get a position as an editor in the white publishing world (even after proposing to white companies that she would be willing to work at home to avoid integrating the workplace). Yet this brilliant woman with the highest credentials and qualifications did not let racism prevent her from making her mark.

Jessie Redmon Fauset and her husband, Herbert F. Harris, a businessman whom she married in 1929, lived in Montclair, New Jersey. When Fauset's husband died in 1958, she moved to Philadelphia and lived there with a relative until her death in 1961.

Zora Neale
HURSTON

(1891–1960)

✦

Atragedy in the careers of many artists is that their work may not generate enough income to support them during their lifetime. Zora Neale Hurston, the best-known female author of the Harlem Renaissance, is a classic example. She never earned as much as $1,000 in royalties during her entire life, but today her books earn thousands of dollars each year. Her name and her talent are now recognized and valued. A Zora Neale Hurston writers festival is held annually in Eatonville, Florida, the town where she was born.

✦An **advance** is money paid to an author for work not yet published.

✦**Royalties** are payments made to an author for each copy of her or his published work sold.

The seventh of eight children of the Reverend John and Lucy Potts Hurston, Zora grew up in Eatonville. In those days, it was an all-black town. When Hurston lost her mother at age thirteen, she was passed around among a series of relatives. It was a situation that made her grow up quickly and become fiercely independent as she took

different odd jobs. One of those jobs was as a traveling maid to an actress with the Gilbert and Sullivan Company. A dramatic personality in her own right, Hurston worked her way to Washington, D.C., where she sporadically attended Howard University and wrote short stories.

While studying at Howard, she had her first short story published. She later studied folk art and anthropology at Barnard College in New York City and is recorded as its first black graduate. Meantime, she continued writing stories.

New York City was the home of the Harlem Renaissance, which produced a vast body of work by black writers in the 1920s. Hurston became closely acquainted with many of the leading black literary figures of the day, including Langston Hughes. Hurston's short stories and novels expressed her feelings about the black community. For example, *Color Struck* addressed the theme of color bias. It is the story of a dark-skinned woman who goes mad because she cannot believe that a man can love someone of her complexion. Hurston, herself of a lovely brown hue, recalled in her 1942 autobiography, *Dust Tracks on a Road*, that as a child she felt confusion about black pride. She remembered thinking, "If it was so honorable and glorious to be black, why was it the yellow-skinned people among us had so much prestige?" As far back as first grade, she recalled the light-skinned children were always chosen for the good parts of fairies and angels.

Hurston also wrote about the ways people could be blinded by greed. In her short story "The Gilded Six Bits," a con artist comes to a small town and dazzles a woman with fake gold. Money also figured in her most celebrated novel, *Their Eyes Were Watching God* (1937).

Written in poetic black dialect, *Their Eyes Were Watching God* tells of love and tragedy in the life of Janie Crawford, a bride of sixteen. Janie, who lives in a small southern town very much like the one in which Zora was raised, is forced into an unloving marriage by her grandmother, who feels she knows what is best for her granddaughter. Having had to struggle all her life, Janie's grandmother is only

The poet Langston Hughes was a leading figure in the Harlem Renaissance. His poetry painted vivid images of African American life. Collaborating with Hurston, he wrote the play Mule Bone.

concerned with wealth. She readily dismisses Janie's views about romance and insists that her granddaughter marry an elderly man. The novel ends with Janie eventually finding true love in the character of Tea Cake, a spirited young man, who she describes as being like "a bee to a blossom."

Today, this novel has sold more than a million copies, and in 1990 was bought by television personality Oprah Winfrey and musician Quincy Jones for film production. But in the 1930s, not everyone

appreciated Hurston's talent. In a period when the black elite thought the black race had to look upright and dignified, Hurston, in their opinion, was not helping their cause. They accused her of representing a "circuslike" side of black life. She was accused of taking advantage of ordinary black people by telling humorous stories about their lives to make white people laugh. Critics also accused Hurston of making light of the harshness of southern black life.

Hurston ignored her critics and held on to her beliefs. In later years, Zora Neale Hurston was one of the few voices to dare question the soundness of the 1954 U.S. Supreme Court *Brown* v. *Board of Education* decision, which declared segregated schools unconstitutional. Recalling her own education in Eatonville, Hurston argued that a black child didn't necessarily need to be seated next to a white student to learn well. White segregationists welcomed the position she took, while blacks distanced themselves from her. Blacks felt that comments like Hurston's could only hurt their cause.

Critics in the black press also wrote harsh stories about her personal life. Distanced from family members, Hurston was without close support. With her few financial resources, including a $500 advance for her next book, the beleaguered writer returned to Florida. Once these funds were depleted, Zora Neale Hurston, a woman accustomed to making her own way in the world, took a job as a maid. Hurston's employers discovered that their maid, whom they referred to as "the girl," was the same person they saw in a magazine. They reported the story to the *Miami Herald*. When Hurston was called on to respond, embarrassment caused her to lie and say that she was working as a maid to gather research.

She was twice married and divorced. She explained to friends that marriage had stood in the way of her writing. She is reported to have had a long and serious relationship with a young man, who may have been her one true love, and who perhaps was the inspiration for the fictional character of Tea Cake. Despite her devotion to him, however,

the relationship did not last. Like many writers, she opted for "the solitary life," a subject she addresses in her autobiography. She writes, "I have come to know by experience that work is the nearest thing to happiness that I can find." Zora felt destined to be a loner. "I played, fought, and studied with other children," she recalls, "but always stood apart."

Though she was described in her final years as "a poor woman living in a dilapidated building where she paid $5.00 per week," her correspondences to her publisher suggest that she remained optimistic. In one of her letters, she told her editor, "I am living the kind of life for which I was born, strenuous and close to the soil." The book she was working on for Scribners was rejected, but Hurston did not give up. After moving to Cocoa, Florida, she attempted to revise the book. Later she moved to Fort Pierce, where she worked as a librarian and teacher. In 1959, a stroke forced her to enter Fort Lucie County Welfare Home, where she died on January 28, 1960, at age sixty-nine.

IN SEARCH OF ZORA

Zora Neale Hurston's writings were reintroduced to the public by the contemporary writer Alice Walker. A native southerner herself, Walker closely identified with Hurston's stories and waged a passionate one-woman campaign to unearth and bring to light the writings of Zora Neale Hurston and other black women writers who were simply out of print. She wrote numerous articles about the author's personal struggle as an artist. She lectured about the life and work of Hurston and eventually produced the book *I Love Myself When I Am Laughing: A Zora Neale Hurston Reader* (1979). An article written for *Ms.* magazine, "In Search of Zora Neale Hurston" (1975), resulted in an outpouring of interest in the writer.

While searching the backlands of Florida in 1973, Alice Walker found Hurston's grave in an isolated weeded area. At the site of the author's grave, she placed a headstone that reads "A Genuis of the South."

DOROTHY
WEST

(1907–1998)

✦

"Your pioneering achievements have made you a role model for independent women," a telegram from television personality Oprah Winfrey read. Professor Henry Louis Gates of Harvard was in attendance along with his colleague Cornel West and numerous other luminaries and special guests. Opera singer Jessye Norman had come to sing. Author Jill Nelson was there to read, and First Lady Hillary Rodham Clinton brought greetings from President Bill Clinton. The place was Martha's Vineyard, an island off the coast of Massachusetts, and the special occasion was the ninetieth birthday of author Dorothy West, whose writing career spanned more than seventy years.

Dorothy, the only child of Rachel Pease and Isaac Christopher West, was born in Boston, Massachusetts, on June 1, 1907. Her father was a former slave who established a successful fruit and vegetable business that moved his family into Boston's black upper-middle class. Dorothy's mother was a lively, attractive woman who was some years younger than her husband. She brought as many as eighteen of her siblings to live with her in the elegant four-story house where she,

her husband, and daughter resided. Helen Johnson, a niece who was the same age as Dorothy, was also part of the Wests' extended household.

Dorothy was educated at Girl's Latin School and graduated at age sixteen. She then attended Boston University and the Columbia School of Journalism. West began writing short stories at age seven and had her stories published in the *Boston Post* by age fifteen. She and her cousin Helen Johnson, along with other young black aspiring writers, formed the Saturday Evening Quill Club in Boston. In 1926, at age eighteen, Dorothy won second prize from the Urban League magazine *Opportunity* for the short story "The Typewriter." The young author and her cousin moved to New York, where they became part of the Harlem Renaissance arts movement. Though Helen never reached the level of success her cousin Dorothy attained, she was also a published author.

Upon arriving in New York, Dorothy was taken under the wing of Zora Neale Hurston, with whom she shared second place in the writing contest. Hurston was highly impressed with the young artist,

LIVING INSIDE A STORY

The extended family that West grew up in was common among black families regardless of their economic status. This family structure assured that nearly all the children in the family had male and female influences and close supervision. In Dorothy's essay "My Mother, Rachel West," she describes her early years: "The house I grew up in was four-storied. We were an extended family, continuously adding new members and the joke was, if we lived in the Boston Museum, we'd still need more room. Surrounded by all these different personalities, each one wanting to be first among equals, I knew I wanted to be a writer. Living with them was like living inside a story."

and the two eventually shared an apartment. Through this friendship, West met literary figures such as the novelist and editor Wallace Thurman, and the poets Langston Hughes and Countee Cullen. Nicknamed "the kid" by Langston Hughes, West recalled being shy and seldom speaking out in the circle of literary giants, but she was delighted to be in their company. Later, she reminisced, "We were all young and we fell in love with each other. We all had the same ambitions: writers and painters and so forth. We had an innocence that nobody can have now."

In 1932, Dorothy West traveled to Russia along with Langston Hughes and twenty other African Americans to make a film about

Talented African American writers and artists such as (clockwise, from lower right to upper right) Langston Hughes, Margaret Walker, Zora Neale Hurston, Sterling Brown, Robert Hayden, Owen Dodson, Jacob Redick, Melvin B. Jolson, Arna Bontemps, and many others began one of the most creative and exciting periods in American history: the Harlem Renaissance.

Color and Class

Dorothy West's upper-class upbringing served as background for much of her first novel, *The Living Is Easy* (1948), as well as for the novel *The Wedding* (1995), which became a television movie, and for a collection of short stories and autobiographical essays, *The Richer, the Poorer* (1995).

In *The Living Is Easy*, the main character, Cleo Judson, like Dorothy West's mother, is light-skinned and has a dark-skinned daughter in whose life she is overly involved. West highlights the color and class differences in black families like the one she grew up in, and the pain it caused so many. It was probably a subject that she and her good friend Zora Neale Hurston spent considerable time discussing, since Hurston also explored this issue in her work.

race relations, but the film never materialized. She returned to the United States in 1934 upon learning of her father's death.

The Harlem Renaissance had faded with the onset of the Great Depression, the severe economic crisis of the 1930s. Ever since the stock market crashed in 1929, Americans had struggled to make a living. Employment was difficult to find. West accepted a small role as a stage actor. She later worked briefly as a welfare investigator, a job that became the source of many of her short stories. She was paid $50 per story by the New York *Daily News* for publication of her short stories. She once won $400 for a story.

Dorothy West eventually became part of the WPA Writers Project. Launched in 1935, the Work Projects Administration (WPA), a U.S. government agency established under President Franklin Roosevelt, put 8 million people back to work. Among them were many talented black writers, including John Johnson, who became editor and publisher of *Ebony*, the longest-established black magazine.

In 1935, Dorothy West began her own magazine, *Challenge*, a literary quarterly. The last issue of *Challenge* appeared in 1937. It was

replaced with *New Challenge*, a more political version of the original magazine. West served as editor along with Richard Wright, who also became a famous writer. In her role as editor, she encouraged writers to submit stories that addressed the struggle of poor and working-class people.

In the 1940s, West wrote columns for the *Vineyard Gazette* of Massachusetts while she was caring for elderly relatives on Martha's Vineyard. She lived in a cedar-shingled cottage in Oak Bluff, which had been bought by her father and where she had spent many summers as a child. She loved the island: "I have lived in various places, but the island is my yearning place. All my life, wherever I have been, abroad, New York, Boston, anywhere, I yearned for home, I yearned for the island."

Once settled on the island, she slowly started working on another novel. She worked on it for more than forty years. Jacqueline Kennedy Onassis, a book editor and a neighbor, traveled to the cottage weekly during the summer to work directly with West on the book. They decided to call it *The Wedding*. The novel, which became a best-seller, was praised for giving a glimpse inside a world that few outsiders, black or white, previously knew existed. West dedicated the award-winning novel to the memory of Mrs. Onassis, who died shortly before its publication. Until Dorothy West died at age ninety-one in Boston, she was the last surviving member of the Harlem Renaissance.

A N N
PETRY

(1911–1997)

✦

Millions of African Americans from the South headed to northern cities in the early decades of the twentieth century. People left home in search of work and to escape Jim Crow laws of segregation. This "great migration" frequently led to Harlem. Newly arrived southerners viewed it and other northern cities as "the promised land." Author Ann Petry was the first African American woman to tell their story.

Born in 1911, the author grew up in Old Saybrook, Connecticut. Her father owned a pharmacy in which several members of Petry's maternal family worked as pharmacists. Petry also completed pharmacy school and worked in her father's business for a while. As a high school student, Ann received praise from a teacher for her writing. This encouraged her to submit stories to magazines for publication. Although these early attempts proved fruitless, she did not lose faith, but continued to search for writing opportunities. She was soon hired to write advertising copy for the New York *Amsterdam News*. Later she became a reporter and an editor for the *People's Voice*, a weekly news-

61

paper in Harlem, owned by pastor and politician Adam Clayton Powell Jr.

When Petry began submitting material to magazines again, her work was accepted by the NAACP magazine *Crisis*. Editors of the Houghton Mifflin publishing company discovered her short story "Like a Winding Sheet" (1945). The NAACP's magazine paid Petry only the small sum of $20 for her story, but the exposure she received from its publication launched her career. She received a $2,500 literary prize and a contract from Houghton Mifflin. Petry's short story eventually grew into her first novel, *The Street* (1946). It was the first novel by an African American to sell a million copies.

The main character in *The Street* is Lutie Johnson, who struggles to raise her son Bub in a 1920s Harlem neighborhood. Lutie Johnson has dreams of a better life but continues to meet obstacles as she tries to get ahead. Not only is the plight of this single parent a difficult one, but so are the situations of most of the people around her. Petry vividly captures the spirit of the Harlem neighborhood, where recent arrivals from the South are trying to adjust to city life. There are the struggling maids and other blue-collar workers whose faces show the

WHY DO WRITERS WRITE?

In an interview for *Crisis* magazine, Ann Petry listed reasons why she wrote *The Street*. She said that she wanted first to show how environment can change a person's life. She also wanted to explain the cause of high crime and death rates in black communities. She wanted to demonstrate the breakdown of black family life in northern urban areas. And finally, she wanted to show that black people had the same emotions and capacity for love, hate, tears, and laughter as any other group of people.

strain of their lives. There are city-slick hustlers who seek innocent souls to prey upon. And there are the many latchkey children who, like Lutie's son Bub, are left on their own.

Although Ann Petry was not born in Harlem, she knew it well. She moved there after she married George David Petry in 1938. Her work as a local journalist and an instructor in an after-school program gave her daily encounters with many transplanted southerners. Petry's husband was also from the South, so she had no difficulty learning southern speech patterns. The author, who studied creative writing at Columbia University in New York, also took courses in psychology and psychiatry, which helped her to understand people and develop believable characters.

The Street was followed by two more novels, *Country Place* (1947), which focused on marital difficulties, and *The Narrows* (1953), the story of an interracial romance. Ann Petry also wrote stories for children and young adults, including two biographies: *Tituba of Salem Village*, and *Harriet Tubman, Conductor of the Underground Railroad*. Petry was a member of the American Negro Theater and lectured at major universities, including the University of California at Berkeley and the University of Miami in Florida. She was also a visiting professor of English at the University of Hawaii.

With the reissue of *The Street* in 1992 by the Feminist Press, the novelist gained new fame and her work was taught widely in schools. In the spring of 1997, an audience of fans and literary personalities, including author-actress Ruby Dee, gathered at the Manhattan Theater Club to celebrate the fiftieth anniversary of *The Street*. Ann Petry was ill and could not attend the event, so her daughter, Elizabeth, came on her behalf.

Shortly after this, Ann Petry died at age eighty-six in Old Saybrook, where she and her husband had returned many years earlier.

ANOTHER NOTED WRITER IN THE NEW CENTURY

Alice Moore Dunbar-Nelson (1875–1935) was born Alice Ruth Moore in New Orleans to middle-class Creole parents, Joseph and Patricia Moore. She attended local public schools and graduated from the two-year teaching program at Straight College (now Dillard University). She continued her studies at the University of Pennsylvania, Cornell University, and the School of Industrial Arts in Pennsylvania, where she majored in psychology and English. She was an accomplished violinist, cellist, mandolin player, amateur actress, and writer.

Moore's first book was a collection of poems, titled *Violets and Other Tales* (1895). Upon reading the title poem "Violet," Paul Laurence Dunbar, an older established poet, was charmed by the following lines:

> I had not thought of violets of late;
> The wild, shy kind that spring beneath your feet
> In wistful April days, when lovers mate;
> And wander through the field in raptures sweet . . .

Dunbar's admiration led to a correspondence between the two writers and eventually to their marriage in 1898. They were divorced in 1902.

The author's second book, *The Goodness of St. Rocque* (1899), was also a collection of poems, sketches, and short stories. She also wrote extensively on race and women's issues. She wrote for the *Wilmington* [Delaware] *Advocate* and other national black publications, including the *Pittsburgh Courier*, the *Washington Eagle*, the *New York Sun* and the *Chicago Daily News*. She also served as co-editor of the *African Methodist Episcopal Review*.

Alice Moore Dunbar-Nelson left her diaries and unpublished manuscripts with her relatives for safekeeping before her death in 1935. These treasured writings—several novels, short stories, plays, poetry, and essays, and a diary that chronicled her relationships with such notables as Langston Hughes, James Weldon Johnson, George Douglas Johnson, W. E. B. Du Bois, and Mary McLeod Bethune—were found about fifty years later in the attic of a relative.

Alice Moore Dunbar-Nelson was also a noted teacher and activist who ceaselessly championed the rights of blacks and women.

MODERN TIMES

MARGARET WALKER
ALEXANDER

(1915–1998)

Jubilee (1966), the sweeping historical novel written by Margaret Walker Alexander, was based on stories she heard from her grandmother, whose mother was a slave. Unlike Margaret Mitchell's popular novel *Gone With the Wind*, in *Jubilee* there are no "happy slaves." One hundred years after emancipation, black Americans welcomed the book. They were ready for a different view of the Civil War.

Margaret Walker was fortunate in having a grandmother who was willing to tell her about slavery. Many older blacks refused to share their memories because the experience of slavery was a source of shame for them. So they stopped discussing it, as though it had never happened. But Margaret Abigail Walker's grandmother was not about to forget. Margaret's father would sometimes suggest that her grandmother was "making up tales." Her grandmother would then promptly respond that she wasn't making up anything, but was telling the child the "naked truth."

Born in Birmingham, Alabama, to Sigismund C. Walker, a Methodist minister, and Marion Dozier Walker, a music teacher, Margaret

was reared in a home where education was valued. Her talent was encouraged at an early age. She wrote her first poems as a pre-teen. At first, her father dismissed her efforts, but he later gave her a date book and suggested that she record her poetry in it. Young Margaret set a goal to fill all the pages, which she did by the time she turned eighteen. By then, she was a junior in college. She wrote every day.

In addition to the encouragement she received from her parents, Margaret also received recognition and encouragement from one of her teachers, Miss Fluke, who recognized that young Margaret's skills far exceeded those of her peers. She suggested to the Walkers that they make an attempt to get their exceptional daughter out of the small segregated black school and into an arena where there would be greater challenges. The poet Langston Hughes later visited New Orleans and made the same assessment of Margaret's achievements.

At age fifteen, the brilliant young student was sent to Northwestern University in Evanston, Illinois. While studying there, Walker met Dr. W. E. B. Du Bois, who published her first poem in *Crisis* magazine when she was eighteen. Her favorite teacher, Professor Edward Buell Hungerford, helped expand Walker's knowledge of the

WHAT INFLUENCES A WRITER MOST?

Margaret Walker attributed much of her creative genius to her parents who taught at what is now Dillard University in New Orleans, Louisiana. She recalls: "Whether the music was classical—Bach, Beethoven, and Brahms—church hymns or anthems, folk songs such as spirituals, work songs, blues, or ragtime and popular ballad and jazz, I heard music, my mother's music, as my earliest memory. My images have always come from the southern landscape of my childhood and adolescence. The meaning or philosophy came from my father, from his books and from his sermons. Most of all it came from reading the Bible."

techniques and forms of poetry. It was in Hungerford's class that she began the first draft of her masterpiece novel *Jubilee*. She did not know it at the time, but Professor Hungerford waged a one-man battle against racism to have her admitted to the Poetry Society of America.

Graduating from Northwestern in 1935 during the Depression, Margaret searched in vain for employment. After seven months, she began to work with the WPA Chicago Writers Project, where she held a variety of jobs, including typist and newspaper reporter. While working for the WPA, she met author Richard Wright. She was impressed with his talent and ambition and the two became close friends. She became part of the Chicago Renaissance, a literary movement that grew out of a South Side writers group, which was led by Richard Wright.

The author completed her famous poem "For My People" (1937) at age twenty-two. "For My People," along with twenty-six other poems by the author, were collected in a book. It received the Yale Series for Younger Poets Award in 1942, making Walker the first African American recipient in the award's history. Continuing her education, she earned a master's degree at the University of Iowa in 1940 and a doctorate in 1965. Margaret Walker married Firnist James Alexander in 1943 and had four children. Her husband became disabled, and she supported the family by teaching school in South Carolina and Mississippi. As a professor at Jackson State College in Mississippi, she established a black studies program. Walker retired from the university as a professor emeritus of English. She was the recipient of numerous literary awards and honors, including a Rosenwald Fellowship and the City University of New York's Langston Hughes Award. She received the Outstanding Lifetime Achievement Award at the International Black Women's Conference held at New York University in November 1997.

Walker's published works include *For My People* (1942), *Jubilee* (1966), *Prophets for a New Day* (1970), *How I Wrote Jubilee* (1972), *October*

Author Richard Wright wrote important social novels about African American life such as Black Boy *and* Native Son.

Journey (1973), *A Poetic Equation: Conversations Between Nikki Giovanni and Margaret Walker* (1974), *For Farish Street Green* (1988), *This Is My Century* (1988), *The Daemonic Genius of Richard Wright* (1988), and *On Being Black, Female and Free* (1997), a collection of essays.

Margaret Walker Alexander died on November 30, 1998, at the home of her daughter Marion Colmon in Chicago, Illinois. Alferdteen

Harrison, director of the Institute for the Study of History, Life and Culture of Black People (founded by Walker at Jackson State University in 1968), said of the famed author, "She was our model, our mentor. . . . She showed the way. That was the mark of greatness."

ON BEING HUMAN

Margaret Walker lived in the South during the turbulent sixties. Her neighbor, civil rights leader Medgar Evers, was assassinated on the street where she lived. Yet, reflecting on the injustices she has seen in life, Walker observed, "I taught my students that every person is a human being. Every human personality is sacred, potentially divine. Nobody is any more than that and nobody can be less . . ."

GWENDOLYN
BROOKS

(B. 1917)

◆

In 1950, Gwendolyn Brooks became the first African American woman to win the Pulitzer Prize for poetry for her book *Annie Allen*. It was an accomplishment that brought her wide acclaim. With Jim Crow segregation laws still in place in the South and "de facto" (unwritten but practiced) segregation in the North, her stardom was celebrated by all African Americans.

Gwendolyn Brooks was born June 7, 1917, in Topeka, Kansas, to David Anderson and Keziah Corinne Wims Brooks. Her father was a janitor and her mother taught school. Brooks began writing poetry as early as age eleven, and had her first poem published in *American Child* magazine at age fifteen. She received encouragement in her poetry from the noted poet and novelist James Weldon Johnson through correspondences she had with him. While in high school, Brooks contributed articles to a column in the *Chicago Defender* newspaper. She graduated in 1935 and enrolled in Wilson College the following year. Brooks worked briefly as a secretary in Chicago and served as publicity director for the NAACP Youth Council. She met

PHOTO BY BILL TAGUE

Henry Lowington Blakely, the man who would become her husband, at one of the NAACP Youth Council meetings. The couple were married in 1939 and have two children.

Brooks joined a local Chicago poetry workshop in 1940, where she polished her craft. The poet's writing came to the attention of an editor from the Knopf Publishing Company after she won the Midwestern Conference Poetry Award in 1943. Brooks gave the Knopf editors a sampling of her work, which ranged from poems about love to poems on racial prejudice. The editors requested that she send more "Negro" poems. Uncomfortable with their request, she decided to submit a selection of her work to editors at Harper and Row Publishers instead. They became the publisher of her first book, *A Street in Bronzeville* (1945). This was followed by publication of *Annie Allen* (1949), *Maude Martha* (1953), and *The Bean Eaters* (1968), all Harper publications.

Maude Martha provides one of the few glimpses into urban black life during and after World War II from a woman's point of view. Maude has come to terms with the racism she has known as a child and as an adult. But she finds it difficult to watch it spread to yet another generation. Brooks creates a Christmas scene where Maude Martha has taken her little girl, Paulette, to visit Santa Claus. While Santa shakes hands and fusses over the white children before him, he refuses even to make eye contact with Paulette. Angered by Santa's

WRITE ABOUT WHAT YOU KNOW

Gwendolyn Brooks's first novel, *Maude Martha*, is told from the point of view of a Chicago housewife and closely resembles the writer's own life. When talking about the book, Brooks states: "I didn't want to write about somebody who turned out to be a star 'cause most people don't turn out to be stars. And yet their lives are just as sweet and just as rich as any others and often they are richer and sweeter."

attempt to make her child invisible, Maude speaks up, "Mister, my little girl is talking to you. . . ." Later, she tries to convince Paulette that she was not being ignored and that Santa loves her just as much as he does white children.

It was while attending a writers conference in 1967, at the historically black Fisk University, that Brooks encountered her first group of young "black literary revolutionaries." These young people were convinced that black writers had a key role to play in the civil rights movement that was in progress. Gwendolyn Brooks and other older writers arrived at the conference totally unprepared for their reception from the militant young writers, who challenged them to re-examine their literary careers. Lerone Bennett, a black historian and editor of *Ebony* magazine, heard their complaints about the magazine's advertisements of bleaching creams and the almost exclusive use of light-skinned blacks in their advertisements.

Brooks was challenged to make her verse more relevant to "the struggle" and more accessible to the masses. Young black writers who were actively engaged in the civil rights movement saw people like Lerone Bennett and Gwendolyn Brooks as figures who could help advance the cause of civil rights. Young writers felt that established writers could use their positions and talents to speak out against injustices against blacks.

In summarizing the conference, Brooks wrote: "I arrived in Nashville, Tennessee, to give one more 'reading.' But a blood-boiling surprise was in store for me. First, I was aware of a general energy, and electricity, a look, gesture of the young blackness I saw all about me." Brooks maintained an open mind to the comments and concerns of the students she met. She says that the young people she met in the 1960s educated her. "They gave me books to read. We talked. They just absorbed me, adopted me."

When Brooks returned to Chicago, she established networks with younger writers. She formed a workshop for aspiring writers. She and

the young people found new ways to do just what the Fisk students had suggested. They *took* the poetry to the people in neighborhood parks, in churches, on street corners, and even in bars. The Black Stone Rangers, a Chicago street gang, were among the young people Brooks reached out to through the sharing of poetry. She urged them and other young people to stay in school and get an education, and sometimes used her poetry to say it.

A significant and surprising career change occurred when Gwendolyn Brooks made the decision to leave her commercial publisher, Harper and Row, and place her new works with independent black publishers Broadside and Third World Press. Her faith in and love for these small black publishing companies gained her tremendous respect among young African Americans. Small black presses could in no way offer Brooks the income, publicity, or sales that a major publishing company like Harper and Row could. Still, she remained successful.

Throughout her writing career, Brooks has taught writing at various colleges and lectured around the country. She received numerous honors, including the American Academy and Institute of Arts and Letters Award, a Guggenheim Fellowship, and honorary doctoral

WHAT INSPIRES YOU?

Gwendolyn Brooks took much of her inspiration from everyday life. The city of Chicago, like New York, was a final destination for blacks who continued to leave the South in search of better lives. They came north with their stories and made new ones every day. Commenting on her inspiration, Brooks once said, "If you wanted a poem, you had only to look out the window. There is always material . . ."

degrees. She followed Carl Sandburg as poet laureate of Illinois in 1968 and served for sixteen years.

Among her later publications are *Selected Poems* (1963), *In the Mecca* (1968), *Riot* (1970), *Family Pictures* (1971), *Aloneness* (1971), *The World of Gwendolyn Brooks* (1971), *Report from Part One* (1972), *The Tiger Who Wore Gloves* (1974), *Beckonings* (1975), and *To Disembark* (1981). She also served as editor for *A Broadside Treasury* (1971) and *Jump Bad* (1971).

Throughout her professional career, Gwendolyn Brooks has been a teacher and a mentor to many students and has annually awarded prize money to beginning poets. She resides in Chicago. In November 1997, writers from around the country gathered at the University of Chicago to honor her on her eightieth birthday.

MAYA
ANGELOU

(B. 1928)

One of the most versatile writers in American history is poet and novelist Maya Angelou. Her accomplishments as a dancer, singer, producer, composer, actor, teacher, and writer have brought her international acclaim.

She was born Marguerite Annie Johnson on April 4, 1928, in St. Louis, Missouri, to Vivian Banter and Bailey Johnson. She had a younger brother who was also named Bailey. After their parents' divorce, young Margaret and her brother were raised primarily by their paternal grandmother, Annie Henderson, in Stamps, Arkansas. Years later, they went to live with their mother in San Francisco.

Angelou tells of her childhood experiences in her first memoir, *I Know Why the Caged Bird Sings* (1970). She describes what life was like for a black girl in the South during the 1930s.

✦A **memoir** is another type of autobiography.

A National Book Award nominee, the highly praised autobiography remains a best-seller thirty years later and has been adapted for television.

Maya Angelou graduated from Mission High School in San Francisco at age sixteen and gave birth to a son shortly thereafter. As a young single parent, she struggled in a variety of jobs, ranging from short-order cook to nightclub dancer. She attributes her ability to survive this most difficult period to the upbringing and examples of her grandmother, who was also a survivor. The author tells of early childhood lessons from her grandmother and about her own struggles as a young mother in her second memoir, *Gather Together in My Name* (1974). By the time she wrote *Making Merry Like Christmas* (1976), the third book of the autobiographical series, she is married and divorced. The author would marry and divorce twice more. In this same time period (the 1950s), Angelou traveled and performed in the European production of the opera *Porgy and Bess*. It was a time of great possibilities for her, but since she had to return to the United States to raise her son, her tour with the production ended.

Angelou later moved to New York, where she became associated with artists involved with the civil rights movement of the 1960s. One of them was author John O. Killens, co-founder of the Harlem Writers Guild. She also met James Baldwin, Paule Marshall, Rosa Guy, and many other literary figures. This period of her life is covered in her fourth memoir, *The Heart of a Woman* (1981). During the 1970s, the Ghanaian government invited African Americans to join them in Ghana, where they could share their talents. Maya Angelou and other activist artists traveled there to live. Journalist Jean Carey Bond and her architect husband, Max Bond, and artist-illustrator Tom Feelings (with whom Angelou later produced a book of poetry) were among those who responded to the Ghanaian invitation. Angelou's time spent in Africa is detailed in her fifth memoir, *All God's Children Need Traveling Shoes* (1986).

In January 1993, President Bill Clinton asked Maya Angelou to write a poem for his inauguration. This request marked a first for an African American and a first for a woman. Though the request was a

major honor for Angelou, it was not the first time she had been called on by a president of the United States. She was appointed by President Jimmy Carter to the national commission on the observance of International Women's Year, and by President Gerald R. Ford to the American Revolution Bicentennial Advisory Council. At this writing, Angelou is an honorary chairperson with the United Nations Children's Fund (UNICEF).

Beginning with Angelou's 1960s commitment to the civil rights struggle, she has lent her name to many causes involving children and women. At the request of Dr. Martin Luther King Jr., she served as the northern coordinator for the Southern Christian Leadership Conference. This versatile artist has not only worked as an actress but has written, directed, and produced plays for films and television. The author is friend and mentor to television personality Oprah Winfrey. She also advises other artists, including singers and songwriters Nick Ashford and Valerie Simpson, with whom she has produced a song-and-poetry album that they performed at Carnegie Hall in New York City.

BECOMING A BEAUTIFUL PERSON

Angelou has been featured many times in *Essence*, the major black women's publication in this country. Interviewed by *Essence* magazine editor in chief, Susan Taylor, Maya Angelou offered the following advice on becoming a beautiful person:

"Being a host to grace provides one with gentility, a generosity, a spirit of forgiveness and humor. The minute you host grace, you speak slower because you want to be understood. You speak more softly because you don't want to jar, offend, or run anybody away (except those who mean you no good). Your gestures are larger, more open, more generous. People's ideas about you become much less important. And you literally do become more beautiful."

Angelou is proud to be a black woman and celebrates it in her writing and performances. In an introductory essay in the twentieth anniversary issue of *Essence*, she states, "I'm so glad I'm a black woman, because if I were anything else I'd be so jealous." Though she frequently displays a "teasing" side, Angelou is serious about the elevation of black womanhood. In the most popular of her poems, "And Still I Rise," she captures how black women have endured endless hardships and struggles and yet continue to "rise" and walk tall.

I Know Why the Caged Bird Sings is among the all-time best-selling books in the country. Other books by the author are *Just Give Me a Cool Drink of Water 'fore I Die* (1971), *Oh Pray My Wings Are Gonna Fit Me Well* (1975), *And Still I Rise* (1978), *Shaker, Why Don't You Sing?* (1983), and *Wouldn't Take Nothing for My Journey* (1998).

The author has one son and one grandson. She is the recipient of numerous awards and honors and is currently the Reynolds Professor at Wake Forest University in Durham, North Carolina. As of this writing, Maya Angelou is directing films and has homes in North Carolina, New York, and Georgia.

MARSHALL

(B. 1929)

✦

Following World War I (1917–1918) a new group of black people brought their cultures and stories to America. Coming from the Caribbean islands known as the West Indies, they had unique traditions and dialects. And like most immigrants, they came to America seeking jobs and opportunities.

Paule Marshall was born Valenza Pauline Burke to Ada and Samuel Burke on April 9, 1929, the year the stock market crashed. Her parents had come to the United States from Barbados, West Indies, following World War I. She was raised in Brooklyn, New York, in a neighborhood where the population was predominantly immigrants of Caribbean background. After graduation from high school, she attended Brooklyn College where she earned a bachelor of arts in 1953. She continued her studies at Hunter College, earning a master's degree in 1955. She later joined the Harlem Writers Guild.

Her first short story, "The Valley Between," was published in *Our World* magazine in 1954. Her first and best-known novel is *Brown Girl, Brownstones* (1959). It tells the story of Selina Boyce and her West

Indian family who live in Brooklyn, New York. Brownstones are hand-some, look-alike town houses. Many were abandoned by white immigrants as the new black immigrants prospered and moved in. Selina's mother dreams of owning one. Selina's father, on the other hand, longs to return to his beloved Caribbean island.

Black immigrant women like Selina's mother, toiling endlessly to fulfill their dreams in America during World War II (1941–1945), are the main focus in *Brown Girl*. The narrator explains that the "lucky" ones have a regular white woman for whom they work. These black women boarded trains daily to clean homes, cook meals, and care for the children of white women. The Caribbean women without permanent employers had to rise early to stand on street corners where potential employers would look them over in a manner almost as demeaning as a slave auction block.

Many of the women in *Brown Girl, Brownstones* hold two and sometimes three jobs. Marshall describes the workday of Miss Thompson, who is a beautician by day, an office cleaner by night, and the mother of three small children: "At dawn she had eaten in an all-night diner, dozing over her coffee, then as the morning cleared, she had come to the beauty parlor." Pausing to work on a sore foot, Miss Thompson "dresses the ugly unhealed ulcer on the instep of her foot. . . . This done, she leaned back and, for the first time in twenty-four hours since she had been up, permitted herself to feel tired."

Paule Marshall praises the strength of her mother and the other black women of her community in an essay titled "The Making of a Writer: From the Poets in the Kitchen." It was their stories she overheard and delighted in as a young girl in Brooklyn.

Marshall has worked as a librarian, a journalist, and a college professor. She taught literature at major universities including Columbia, Virginia Union, and Yale, and lectured extensively both in the United States and abroad. Paule Marshall has one adult son and lives in New York City, where she teaches at New York University. Annually, she

"POETS IN THE KITCHEN"

Marshall, who poetically captures the voices and nuances of Caribbean speech, describes all the skills she gained by sitting and listening to conversations in her mother's kitchen. Domestic workers talked about their jobs, reminisced about families left behind, joked about employers, and most of all, shared dreams about improving their lot in what they affectionately called "this man's country."

"When people at readings and writers conferences ask me who my major influences were, they are sometimes a little disappointed when I don't immediately name the usual literary giants. True, I am indebted to those writers, white and black, whom I read during my formative years and still read for instruction and pleasure. But they were preceded in my life by another set of giants whom I always acknowledge before all others: the group of women around the table long ago. They taught me my first lessons in the narrative art. They trained my ear. They set a standard of excellence. This is why the best of my work is to be attributed to them; it stands as testimony to the rich legacy of language and culture so freely passed on to me in the wordshop of the kitchen."

holds a forum at NYU at which she introduces newly published authors and their works. Among the young black women writers she has presented in this forum are prize-winning novelists Edwidge Danticat (*Krik? Krak!*) and A. J. Verdelle (*The Good Negress*), authors who also have a love of the vernacular tradition, especially as practiced by women.

◆The **vernacular** is the normal, spoken language of a group or region.

Paule Marshall received the prestigious MacArthur Award in 1992. Commonly called a "genius award," the MacArthur grant is a cash prize given annually by the MacArthur Foundation to individuals who show exceptional talent in their given field. The money is awarded

over a five-year period to allow an artist to pursue his or her work by helping to alleviate concerns about financial obligations. In addition to the MacArthur Award, Marshall has been the recipient of a Guggenheim Fellowship, a Rosenthal Fellowship, a Ford Foundation grant, and numerous other prizes. Marshall's publications also include *Soul Clap Hands and Sing* (1961), *The Chosen Place, The Timeless People* (1969), *Praisesong for the Widow* (1983), *Reena and Other Stories* (1983), and *Daughters* (1991).

CARIBBEAN HERITAGE

Another notable writer of Caribbean heritage is Jamaica Kincaid. She was born Elaine Potter Richardson on May 24, 1949, in St. Johns Antigua, British West Indies. Her mother was a Carib Indian and her father a Dominican. Kincaid began to study photography and wrote for various magazines, including *Ingenue* and the *New Yorker*. Her work includes *At the Bottom of the River* (1983), *Annie John* (1985), *A Small Place* (1988), *Lucy* (1990), *An Autobiography of My Mother* (1996), and *My Brother* (1997). Like Marshall, Kincaid explores the relationships between mothers and daughters.

LORRAINE
HANSBERRY

(1930–1965)

With the debut of *A Raisin in the Sun* at the Barrymore Theater in New York in March 1959, Lorraine Hansberry became the first black woman to have a play produced on Broadway. This dramatization of a typical 1950s urban black family in Chicago captured national attention. And Hansberry, at age twenty-nine, became the youngest American, the fifth woman, and the first black playwright to win the New York Drama Critics Circle Award for best play. The film version also received national acclaim.

> ✦The first performance of a play or show is its **debut**.

Lorraine Vivian Hansberry was born May 19, 1930, in Chicago, Illinois, to Carl and Nancy Perry Hansberry and was the youngest of four children. She grew up in a middle-class setting; her father was a physician and her Uncle Leo Hansberry was a distinguished professor of history at Howard University. The political and social activities of the family exposed Lorraine Hansberry to black luminaries such as Paul Robeson, singer, actor, and social activist; Duke Ellington, musician; and Walter White, writer and one-time leader of the NAACP.

When Lorraine was a young girl of eight, her family experienced a traumatic event that proved to her that neither high economic status nor social status could protect a black family from racism. In the late 1930s, Lorraine Hansberry's father purchased a home in an all-white section of Chicago. The playwright recalls "howling mobs" surrounding the family's house and throwing bricks in protest. "My desperate and courageous mother patrolled our house all night with a loaded German Luger, doggedly guarding her four children, while my father fought the respectable part of the battle in the Washington court." The historic court case, *Hansberry* v. *Lee*, was won by Carl Hansberry in 1940.

A Raisin in the Sun is an honest and moving story of a typical black family of the 1950s. It includes Lena Younger, the grandmother; her college-age daughter, Beneatha; a married son, Walter Lee; and his wife and son. Lena Younger has a dream of purchasing a home with her late husband's insurance money. She has long wanted her family to escape their dark and dingy tenement apartment and move to a place where there is space and light. But Walter has his own dream. Weary from working as a chauffeur, he wants to purchase a liquor store, the last type of business his religious mother would approve of. Walter's wife, Ruth, loves her husband and wants to be supportive of him. She understands his wish to be self-employed, but she also understands her mother-in-law's dream of a nice new home, since she has the very same dream. Ruth tries not to side with either her husband or her mother-in-law, and instead attempts to be a referee between the two. Beneatha lashes out at her brother, Walter, who eventually loses the family's fortune, including the portion that was to pay her medical school expenses.

Two days before the opening of *A Raisin in the Sun*, Lorraine Hansberry wrote her mother about it.

"Mama, it is a play that tells the truth about people, Negroes and life and I think it will help a lot of people to understand how we are

just as complicated as they are—and just as mixed up—but above all, that we have among our miserable and down-trodden ranks—people who are the very essence of human dignity. That is what, after all the laughter and tears, the play is supposed to say. I hope it will make you very proud."

Hansberry first became interested in theater while attending the University of Wisconsin. Unhappy with the school's curriculum, she left and moved to New York in 1950. There she worked as a reporter and later as an associate editor for the black newspaper *Freedom*, published by entertainer and social activist Paul Robeson. Association with the paper led to involvement with various groups that were working for social change in America. It was in one of these integrated groups that Hansberry met Robert Nemiroff, whom she married in 1953. Though they later divorced, the couple maintained a close relationship.

Like Ann Petry, Dorothy West, and many other black women writers, Lorraine Hansberry used the education and advantages her family background gave her to improve racial tolerance in America. With civil rights of blacks still being denied across the country, and government officials stalling efforts to turn the situation around, there was justifiable impatience among black Americans. Hansberry called for human understanding. Nowhere in *Raisin in the Sun* is this intent more clear than when Lena says to Beneatha:

Have you cried for [your brother] today? I don't mean for yourself and for the family 'cause we lost the money. I mean for him; what he been through and what it done to him. . . . When you starts measuring somebody, measure him right, child. Measure him right. Make sure you done taken account what hills and valleys he come through before he got to wherever he is.

Lorraine Hansberry once worked for actor, singer, and social activist Paul Robeson, pictured above.

Tragically, this most promising voice was here only for a short while. Lorraine Hansberry, who captured African American life in a manner that moved not only black people but all peoples struggling for a decent quality of life for themselves, died of cancer in 1965 at age thirty-five. Her death came while her second play, *The Sign in Sidney Brustein's Window*, was still running on Broadway.

A poster of Lorraine Hansberry's 1969 off-Broadway play, To Be Young, Gifted & Black, *celebrates the playwright's talent and the play's long and successful run on the stage.*

TONI
MORRISON

(B. 1931)

✦

In 1993, Toni Morrison became the first African American to receive the Nobel Prize in literature. Her accomplishments, more than any African American writer of the latter half of the twentieth century, have brought international recognition and unquestionable respectability to black writing.

Born Chloe Anthony Wofford on February 18, 1931, in Lorain, Ohio, she was the second in a family of four children. Morrison's parents, George Wofford, a ship welder, and Ramah Willis Wofford, were migrants who left the South seeking a better life for their family. Her father was a native of Georgia and her mother came from Alabama. In the Depression years, George Wofford instilled discipline and a strong work ethic in his daughter. At age thirteen, she had a regular after-school job of cleaning the home of a white woman. Complaining to her father that the work was "too hard," Chloe was told with firmness, "Girl you don't live there. So you go do your work, get your money and come on home." Such sound, commonsense advice not

only guided the author through life but can be heard in the voices of the characters she creates in her novels.

As the second girl, followed by two younger brothers, Chloe felt less than special. Morrison's own description is that she felt she was in "the most anonymous position in the world." Like many other perceptive children who became writers, Morrison became an avid reader. Consuming volumes of European literature at a young age, she read great novelists such as Dostoyevsky, Tolstoy, Gustave Flaubert, and the English writer Jane Austen. Years later, she would observe, "Those books were not written for a little black girl in Lorain, Ohio, but they were so magnificently done that I got them anyway—they spoke directly to me out of their specificity."

Morrison's early ambition, however, was not to be a writer, but a dancer. It was a dream that came from the European literature she read as a girl. But even as young Chloe read literature outside her community experience, her life was being enriched by the black oral tradition within it. She was steeped in this tradition through the stories of the South told by her mother and father and neighbors who had come north to "the promised land." This tradition, which includes the soulful tradition of the black church, is reflected throughout her writing.

Upon completing high school, Toni Morrison attended Howard University in Washington, D.C. During the 1940s and 1950s, students who attended Howard received both an academic education and lessons in the contradictions of black life. At this time and up to the late 1960s, the university was still steeped in color and class consciousness. Skin complexion and family status played a big part in campus life at Howard. Toni Morrison was disturbed by much of what she saw as a student. Many male students established relationships with women based on skin tone, hair texture, wealth, and other such superficialities. Women themselves discriminated against one another, rejecting individuals of darker complexions for membership into cer-

tain social circles. And though the writings of prominent black authors like Langston Hughes and Zora Neale Hurston were available for the asking, they were not taught. This absence of black studies in the curriculum would eventually become the central issue of student protest at Howard during the 1960s.

Morrison's participation in the Howard Players acting group offered her an escape from the pretentiousness of campus life and placed her in the company of people she liked. With acquaintances having difficulty pronouncing the name Chloe, she chose to use the shortened version of her middle name, "Toni." As she traveled across the country and performed with the Howard Players, Toni Morrison's world expanded. Across the South, she saw the impact racism and discrimination had on the lives of black people.

In 1953, she graduated from Howard with a B.A. in English, and in 1955 earned an M.A. in English from Cornell University. Morrison became an English instructor at Texas Southern University in 1957, and later that year, she returned to Howard, her alma mater, to teach English and the humanities. The following year, she married Harold Morrison, an architect of Jamaican heritage. Her first child, Harold Jr., was born in 1962. While in Washington, Morrison was part of a writers workshop. She had joined the workshop out of a need for adult conversation and to share her passion for literature. While in the group, she began a short story that would become the basis for her first novel. Divorced from her husband in 1965, Morrison returned to live with her family in Ohio.

In 1964, Morrison accepted an editorial position with the textbook division of Random House located in Syracuse, New York. Her dream was to eventually land a position in Random House's Manhattan office. Morrison led a quiet and solitary life in Syracuse, and during this time, she returned to the short story she had started in the Washington workshop. The story blossomed into her first novel, *The Bluest Eye* (1970).

Morrison gave birth to a second son, Slade, in 1967, and her dream of becoming an editor in New York was realized that same year. Hired as a senior editor with Random House, she used her position with the company to help advance the publication of books by black authors. In her eighteen-year tenure with Random House, Toni Morrison was instrumental in publishing numerous black women writers, including Toni Cade Bambara, Alice Walker, Angela Davis, June Jordan, and Gayl Jones.

With the debut of *Sula* (1974), her second book, Morrison gained prominence. *Sula* received impressive reviews from national publications. The reviewer for the *New York Times*, however, suggested that Morrison "should write about subjects larger than African American women." This statement brought letters of criticism from such notable black writers as Alice Walker. No one could recall when any other ethnic writer had been told that it was less than legitimate to write

"THE WORK MUST BE POLITICAL"

Morrison challenges her readers. She wants people to "think" and move beyond just being ordinary readers. Though most of her books are written for a mature audience, some are accessible to younger readers. Her books are complex and demand total attention, and lovers of her work have come to understand her seriousness. She states:

"If anything I do, in the way of writing novels (or whatever I write) isn't about the village or the community or about you, then it is not about anything. I am not interested in indulging myself in some private, closed exercise of my imagination that fulfills only the obligation of my personal dreams—which is to say yes, the work must be political. It must have that as its thrust . . . It seems to me that the best art is political and you ought to be able to make it unquestionably political and beautiful at the same time."

exclusively about their particular race. African American authors would rally around Toni Morrison a second time in 1988, when forty-eight black writers and critics wrote a protest letter to the *New York Times* when *Beloved* (1987), Morrison's fourth novel, did not receive the National Book Award. The book later won the Pulitzer Prize.

Other novels that followed *Sula*, a National Book Award nominee, were *Song of Solomon* (1977); *Tar Baby* (1981); *Beloved* (1987), for which she was awarded the Pulitzer Prize; *Jazz* (1992); and *Paradise* (1998). She wrote a play *Dreaming Emmett*, based on the real-life murder in 1955 of a fourteen-year-old Chicago boy, Emmett Till, who was visiting relatives in the South. She served as general editor for *The Black Book* (1974) and for *Race-ing Justice, En-Gendering Power: Essays on Clarence Thomas and the Construction of Social Reality* (1992). She also wrote an extended essay on literary criticism titled *Playing in the Dark* (1992). Toni Morrison is a sought-after speaker and literary reviewer. Her numerous awards and honors include election to the American Academy and Institute of Arts and Letters. She has taught at the State University of New York at Purchase, Yale University, and the State University of New York at Albany. She was a Regent's Lecturer at the University of California at Berkeley and is currently the Robert F. Gooheen Professor of Humanities at Princeton University.

AUDRE
LORDE

(1934–1992)

✦

Audre Lorde, the poet laureate of New York State, chronicled experiences that were rarely written about, especially from a black woman's point of view.

Audre Geraldine Lorde was born in Harlem, New York, to a Grenadan mother, Linda Belmat, and an African American father, Frederick Byron. As a young child, she had difficulty learning to talk and did not speak until age five. Her speech problem was only fully corrected in adulthood when she traveled to the National University of Mexico in 1954. It was at that time she began speaking in full sentences.

As a young girl, Lorde attended Catholic school, and at age fifteen had her first poem, which was about love, published in *Seventeen* magazine. She enrolled at Hunter College in 1951, and while studying for her degree, worked as an X-ray technician, a factory worker, and at numerous other jobs to support herself. She earned a B.A. in literature and philosophy and became an instructor at Hunter, eventually earning the distinction of distinguished professor. While teaching at Hunter College, she met poet Diana Di Prima, who would later

become the editor of her first collection of poems. Lorde earned an M.A. in library science from Columbia University in 1954 and worked as head librarian at the City University of New York for many years. She later taught writing at Tougaloo College in Mississippi. The experience of teaching and living in the South during the height of the civil rights movement also influenced her poetry. Married and divorced, the poet had two children.

"I write for myself and my children and for as many people as possible who can read me," Lorde wrote.

> When I say myself, I mean not only the Audre who inhabits my body, but all those feisty, incorrigible, beautiful black women who insist on standing up and saying *I am* and you can't wipe me out, no matter how irritating I am. . . . What can I share with the younger generation of black women writers in general. . . . I can tell them not to be afraid to feel and not to be afraid to write about it. Even if you are afraid, do it anyway. We learn to work when we are tired, so we can learn to work when we are afraid.

During the 1970s, Lorde described herself as a "black lesbian feminist warrior poet." Despite the high quality of her writing, her work was not widely reviewed. After being diagnosed with breast cancer, she collected more poems in a book titled *The Cancer Journals*, which was published in 1980. The poet said that she felt it was important to document the experience. "For every poem written, there is the bedrock of experience(s) within which the poem is anchored. A molten hot light shines up through the poem from the core of these experiences. This is the human truth that illuminates the poem surrounding the light that makes it come alive."

Lorde eventually moved to the Caribbean, where she completed her final collection of poems, *Undersong: Chosen Poems Old and New* (1992). Lorde's other publications include *The First Cities* (1968); *Cables*

to *Rage* (1970); *From a Land Where Other People Live* (1973), which was nominated for a National Book Award; *The New York Headshop and Museum* (1974), considered by critics to be her most radical work; *Coal* (1976), her first volume to be released by a major publisher; *Between Ourselves* (1976); *The Black Unicorn* (1978), where she used African mythology to explore women's lives; *The Cancer Journals* (1980); *Zami: A New Spelling of My Name* (1982), which was autobiographical and was described by the author as "biomythography" (combining elements of fiction, biography and mythology); *Chosen Poems—Old and New* (1982); and *Our Dead Behind Us* (1987).

Lorde also wrote several collections of essays that were critically acclaimed. *A Burst of Light* (1988) is a collage of essays and journal entries that continues to explore her struggle with cancer; and *Sister Outsider* (1984), considered by many to be her most influential book, expresses her ideas on critical issues of identity, race, and political and personal empowerment.

Audre Lorde gained admirers not only for the genius, honesty, and bravery of her writing, but for her struggle and insistence on justice and equality for all persons. She died of cancer in 1992. At her memorial service, held at the Cathedral of St. John the Divine in New York, black women and men from around the country came to celebrate Lorde's life and work.

LUCILLE
CLIFTON

(B. 1936)

✦

One of the most beloved writers of her generation, Lucille Clifton had six children, all under the age of ten, when her first book was published. She has lived what most people would call an ordinary life, and writes about everyday feelings and experiences.

Born to Samuel I. Sayes, a steel-mill worker, and Thelma Moore Sayes, a laundress, Clifton grew up in Depew, New York. Her parents did not receive a formal education, but her mother wrote poetry that she read to her four children, and her father told them stories of their ancestors. It was her father's stories that Clifton would later draw from when writing her family history in her book *Generations*.

Clifton was successful in tracing her family back to her great-great grandmother, Carolina Donald, born in Dahomey, West Africa, who, along with other family members, was kidnapped by slave traders. Clifton was named for her great grandmother, who was the first woman legally hanged in Virginia. She was hanged for murdering the white father of her only son. Part of Clifton's success in retracing

her family roots came through a distant white relative who contacted the poet.

After completing high school, Lucille Clifton attended Howard University from 1953 to 1955. Unhappy at Howard, she transferred to the State University of New York at Fredonia, but did not complete her studies. She continued to write, however, and in 1958, she married Fred J. Clifton. She worked as a claims clerk for New York State, a position she held for many years. From 1969 to 1970, she was a literature assistant for the U.S. Office of Education in Washington, D.C.

Clifton's first published writing was a short story in *Negro Digest* during the 1960s. When her first book, *Good Times*, was published in 1969, she recalls being happy and proud, but at age thirty-three and with so many small children, says that she was "too busy to take it terribly seriously. As my children have grown up I have been able to travel more and I enjoy public life; I also enjoy the private."

Clifton's writings are characterized by her use of simple, clear language and a strong sense of black pride. She writes in her poem, "For deLawd": ". . . I come from a line of black and goin' on women." Her poetry also acknowledges the elderly and those forgotten by society as illustrated in her poem "Miss Rosie."

The poet has said: "I have never believed that for anything to be valid or true or intellectual, or *deep*, it had to be complex . . . I am not interested if anyone knows whether or not I am familiar with big words. I am interested in trying to render big ideas in a simple way. I am interested in being understood not admired."

Along with simplicity, clarity of language, and a strong sense of black pride, Clifton also uses humor to communicate her ideas to her readers. The author's first book, *Good Times*, is typical of this. *Good Times*, which depicts the strength of inner-city black families through difficult times, was named Best Book of the Year by the *New York Times*. Clifton's award-winning books and poetry for children describe the many issues young people struggle with while growing up.

In praise of the author, noted poet Haki Madhubuti calls her the "quiet warrior," adding that she is "without doubt a family woman whose husband, children, and extended family have represented and played roles of great importance in her life and work." Clifton has taught at Coppin State College, Goucher College, and the American University in Washington, D.C. She has lectured extensively and held poet-in-residence posts at various colleges and universities, including the University of Cincinnati, George Washington University, Fisk University, and Trinity College.

The awards and special honors she has received for her work include a nomination for a Discover Award, Poetry Center (1969); a Pulitzer Prize Committee Citation (1970); a National Endowment for the Arts Fellowship (1972 and 1974); honorable mention for the Jane Addams Award (1979); poet laureate of Maryland (1979); a nomination for a Pulitzer Prize (1980); an honorary doctor of humane letters, Goucher College (1980); and an honorary doctor of humane letters, University of Maryland (1980).

Her publications include: *Good Times* (1969); *Good News About the Earth* (1972); *An Ordinary Woman* (1974); *Generations* (1976); *Two-Headed Woman* (1970); *Good Woman: Poems and a Memoir, 1969–1980* (1987). Her titles for children and young adults are *The Days of Everett Anderson* (1969); *The Black BC's* (1970); *Everett Anderson's Christmas Coming* (1971); *Good, Says Jerome* (1973); *All Us Come Cross the Water* (1973); *Don't You Remember* (1973); *Everett Anderson's Years* (1974); *The Time That Used to Be* (1974); *My Brother Fine and Me* (1975); *Everett Anderson's Friend* (1975); *Amifika* (1977); *Everett Anderson's 1-2-3* (1977); *Everett Anderson's Nine Month Long* (1978); *The Boy Who Didn't Believe in Spring* (1978); *The Lucky Stone* (1979); *My Friend Jacob* (1980); *Sonora Beautiful* (1981).

The poet and author currently teaches at the University of California at Santa Cruz and maintains her home in Baltimore, Maryland.

AN ORDINARY LIFE

"I grew up a well-loved child in a loving family so I have always known that being very poor, which we were, has nothing to do with lovingness or familyness or character or any of that. This doesn't mean that we were content . . . and never worked at having more. It means that we were/are quite sure that we were/are among the best of people and not having money had nothing to do with that. Other people's opinions didn't influence us about that . . . When I write, especially for children, I try to get that across, that being poor or whatever your circumstances, you are capable of being the best of people and that best, as a human, does not come from the outside in, it comes from the inside out."

—Lucille Clifton

TONI CADE
BAMBARA

(1939–1995)

At the memorial service held for Toni Cade Bambara in New York at the Schomburg Center for Research in Black Culture, the poet Sekou Sundiata, a former student of the author, spoke of her with deep affection. He compared her to Malcolm X. He said that just as Malcolm X was the ideal man of his generation, Bambara was the woman all young men loved. Indeed, the writer was universally loved and respected for her brilliance, beauty, and commitment to social justice.

Born in Harlem, New York, on March 25, 1939, Toni Cade Bambara and her brother, Walter, were raised by their mother, Helen Brent Cade. The family lived in various boroughs of New York City, in New Jersey, and at one point they moved to the South. Mrs. Cade was closely involved in her children's education, insisting that they be taught black history. She frequently showed up unannounced to inspect conditions at their schools. "The village," women of Mrs. Cade's community, helped her to raise her children. This spirit of community was instilled in Toni as a young girl and remained with her

113

throughout her lifetime. Her efforts to help others reached beyond the local level when she traveled to Cuba to work with a women's group in 1973 and met with the Women's Union in Vietnam in 1975.

The author consistently defended the right of women to speak their truths. Defending Ntozake Shange, a young playwright who was verbally attacked for her depiction of black men in her play *For Colored Girls Who Have Considered Suicide When the Rainbow Is Enuf*, Bambara said, "The anger, dismay, disappointment, or just sheer bewilderment that many women experience as a way of life in regard to male/female relationships is something we're all going to have to get used to airing. Women are not going to shut up. We care too much about the development of ourselves and our brothers, fathers, lovers, and sons to negotiate a bogus peace."

Bambara would come to the defense of other young African American women writers who were attacked for the issues they addressed in their writings.

Although Bambara graduated from Queens College with degrees in both theater art and English, and studied African fiction, her early professional career did not focus on writing. During the 1960s, she taught at City College of New York, was a social worker at a Harlem welfare center, a program director at Colony House in Brooklyn, and a recreational therapist in the psychiatric ward of Metropolitan Hospital. Her first official writing job was an editorial position at the City College of New York. This position led to the publication of her short stories in periodicals such as the *Massachusetts Review*, *The Liberator*, and *Redbook* during the late 1960s and early 1970s.

With the women's liberation movement at its peak, Bambara participated in many women's consciousness-raising groups, where she made contact with other women writers. Bambara was energized by these associations where women's issues were the focus of discussions. Encouraged by Addison Gayle, a faculty colleague at City College, she organized a collection of writings by black women that

addressed these issues. The result was a groundbreaking anthology titled *The Black Woman*.

> ✦ An **anthology** is a collection of essays, poems, or short stories gathered into one book.

The Black Woman (1970) was a long overdue and welcome addition to feminist literature. This anthology marked the first time that opinions of black women had been brought together and presented in this manner. It was a significant contribution to literature. The jacket alone, with a dark-skinned black woman wearing a crowning afro hairstyle, made it a treasured item for black women. *The Black Woman* became a guidebook for a generation of young black women. Toni Cade Bambara was highly effective as a spokesperson for the book. She was always informative and very natural when she addressed an audience.

The Black Woman anthology was followed by *Tales and Short Stories for Black Folks* (1971), a collection of stories by established writers such as Alice Walker as well as beginning writers from the freshman class Bambara taught at Rutgers University. The author produced two collections of her own short stories: *Gorilla My Love* (1972) and *The Seabirds Are Still Alive* (1977); and wrote one novel, *The Salt Eaters* (1980), which won the American Book Award. She wrote the introduction to *This Bridge Called My Back* (1981), an anthology of women of color edited by Chicana writers Gloria Anzaldúa and Cherrie Moraga; and contributed to *Love Struggle and Change: Stories by Women* (1988), an anthology of Latina and African American women edited by Irene Zahava.

In addition to teaching writing at City College in New York and Rutgers University in New Jersey, the author was a visiting professor at Duke University in North Carolina and served as writer-in-residence at Spelman College in Atlanta, Georgia. She conducted numerous workshops, readings, and lectures at prisons, museums, libraries, and conferences.

The *New York Times* obituary of Toni Cade Bambara, who died in

Philadelphia at age 56 on December 9, 1995, cited the author as a major contributor to black women's literature.

Noted author Toni Morrison, who edited previous books by Bambara, also edited her final work, *Deep Sightings and Rescue Missions: Fiction, Essays, and Conversations*, published after her death. In the foreword, Morrison expresses appreciation for Bambara's talent and creativity, saying that she was a "writer's writer, an editor's writer, and a reader's writer. . . . In fiction, in essays, in conversations, one hears the purposeful quiet of this ever vocal woman; feels the tenderness in this tough Harlem/Brooklyn girl; joins the playfulness of this profoundly serious writer."

THE FILMMAKER

An artist who constantly grew, Toni Cade Bambara worked on adapting many of her short stories for film. One of her major film projects was *The Bombing of Osage Avenue* (1986), a documentary about an alternative-lifestyle group of families fire-bombed by the Philadelphia police to end their occupation of the area because some of their neighbors viewed them as a nuisance. The bombing incident, which involved children and adults, caused widespread protest in the black community. Bambara's decision to make a film on this incident was typical of how she dealt with her outrage. She states, "I work to celebrate struggle; to applaud the tradition of struggle in our community; to bring to center stage all those characters, just ordinary folks on the block, who've been waiting in the wings . . . I want to lift up some usable truth . . . like the fact that the simple act of cornrowing one's hair is radical in a society that defines beauty as blond tresses blowing in the wind."

Nikki
GIOVANNI

(B. 1943)

Television brought black women writers of the late 1960s and early 1970s into America's living rooms. *Soul*, a 1970s public television series, featured many young writers. A frequent guest was popular poet Nikki Giovanni. Her name became a household word.

Born June 7, in Knoxville, Tennessee, she was given the name Yolande Cornelia Giovanni Jr. When she was two months old, her family moved to Cincinnati, Ohio. After completing high school, she attended Fisk University in Tennessee, where she majored in history. Giovanni attended graduate school at the University of Pennsylvania and the Columbia School of Fine Arts.

While studying at Fisk University, Giovanni met John O. Killens and joined the ranks of writers who benefited from his guidance. Recognizing something special in the young writer, Professor Killens encouraged her to submit her work for magazine publication. Giovanni's first article was published in *Negro Digest*. The poet later recalled, "There are probably no words to describe the joy you feel when you see your first words in print."

Nikki Giovanni's first book, *Black Feelings, Black Talk*, was published with financial support from family and friends. She recalled that she "... formed a publishing company, borrowed heavily from family and friends and hired a printer. Luckily there were a number of black bookstores around the country to which you could send books. All were very kind to me and paid me promptly." Young, attractive, and "hip," Nikki Giovanni rapidly became *the* black poet of her generation. She produced fifteen books in twelve years. They included *Black Feelings, Black Talk* (1968); *Black Judgement* (1969); *Black Re-creation* (1970); *Gemini* (1971), an autobiographical essay for which she received the nomination for the National Book Award for poetry; *A Soft Black Song: Poems for Children* (1971); *My House* (1972); *A Dialogue: James Baldwin and Nikki Giovanni* (1972); *Ego Tripping and Other Poems for Young Readers* (1973); *A Poetic Equation: Conversation Between Nikki Giovanni and Margaret Walker* (1974); *The Women and the Men* (1975); and *Cotton Candy on a Rainy Day* (1978).

The public adored the fiery, new, young voice that spoke so bodaciously about whatever subject she chose. Blacks took pride in her outspokenness, and whites found her easier to listen to than some of the more militant voices of the period. Older people were also charmed with the new young poet who produced albums with gospel groups in the background. A child of the South, Giovanni was comfortable with the elderly, having been close to them in her extended family. In one of her poems she speaks fondly of "knowing that her arms will grow flabby with age, as has been the case of her relatives." Her respect for elders led to conversations with the elder writer Margaret Walker. Giovanni also published and televised conversations with veteran author James Baldwin.

She believed writers needed to keep studying and stretching their minds. "How else can I ask people to read my work and listen to me?" she said. "It would have been pointless for a girl from Knoxville, Tennessee, reared in Cincinnati, Ohio, to have lived in New York and

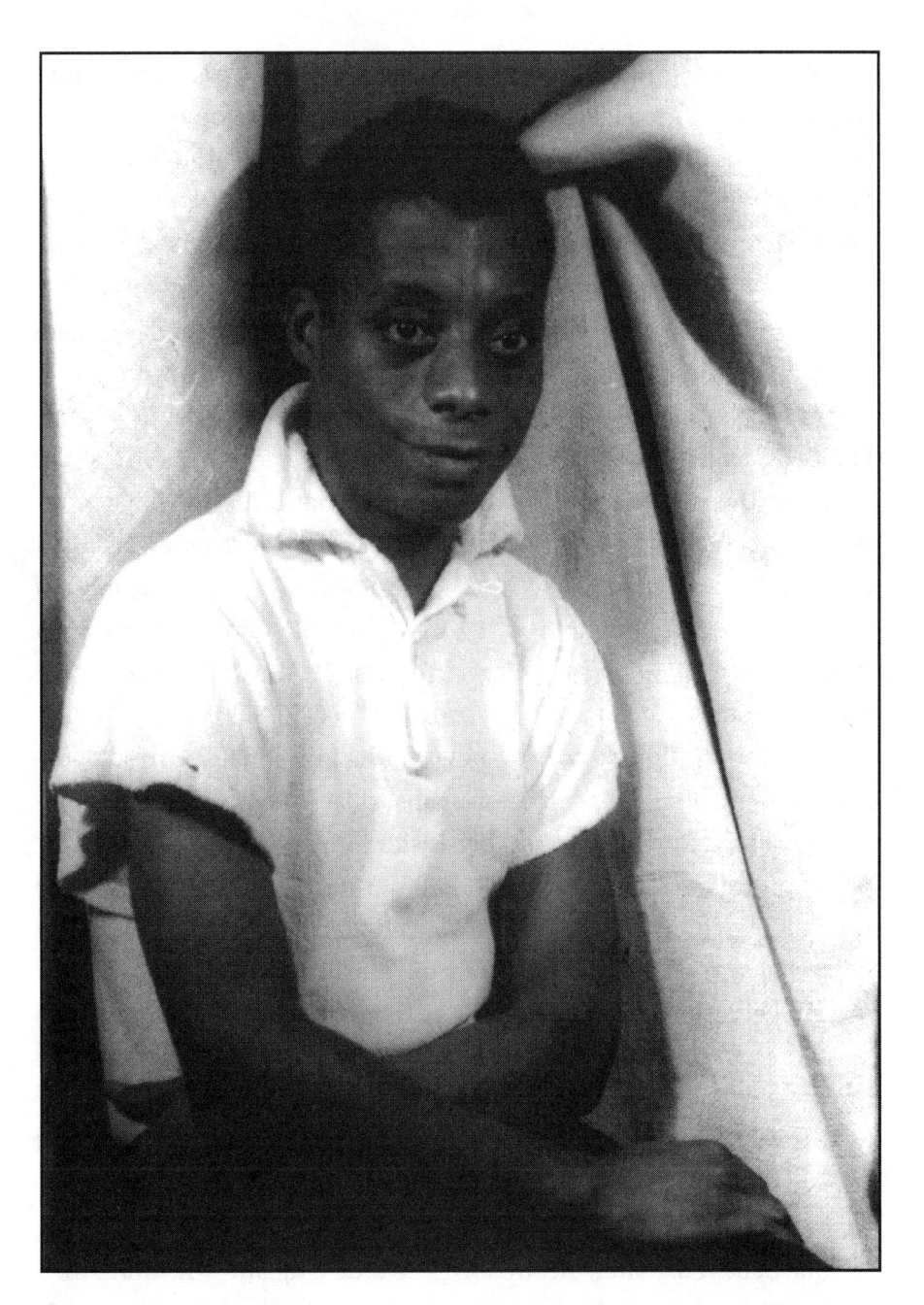

James Baldwin was the author of many novels, short stories, essays, and plays. He was also a leading and outspoken activist for civil rights.

traveled the face of this earth to not have changed. This will have been a betrayal to the trust people put in me as a writer. . . . The only question is of growing up or decaying." This attitude led to some difficult moments. For example, there was the time she decided to travel to South Africa during a boycott by American artists to protest apartheid. This decision caused strain between Giovanni and her acquaintances in the literary community, but in time she was forgiven. In 1997, she received the annual Langston Hughes Award from the City University of New York, an award previously given to writers of stature such as Margaret Walker, Alice Childress, Ralph Ellison, James Baldwin, and her mentor and teacher John O. Killens. The poet also received special recognition from the NAACP in 1998.

Mother of one adult son, the writer contributes frequently to national magazines and scholarly journals and continues to draw a respectable audience wherever she speaks. Giovanni has held academic positions at various universities across the country and is the recipient of honorary doctorates and numerous literary awards. She sparked an interest in poetry for a generation of young people and inspired many of them to write.

ALICE
WALKER

(B. 1944)

✦

Critics have described Alice Walker as the best southern writer of the second half of this century. When reading works of the poet, novelist, short story writer, critic, and essayist, one sees constant reminders of her southern roots permeating her words. The internationally acclaimed author has spoken of the good fortune of writers who have the black southern experience to draw from as they create.

She was born Alice Malsenior Walker on February 9, in Eatonville, Georgia. Her parents, Minnie Lou Grant and Willie Lee Walker, were sharecroppers who had eight children. Sharecropper families tended farms in exchange for poor housing, basic food goods, and inadequate amounts of money. It was a system that generally kept black families in endless debt to white farmers. Parents and children of the family were expected to take part in planting and harvesting crops. Alice Walker's mother also worked as a domestic, but she still found time to sew all her children's clothing and maintain a lovely flower garden.

Alice would pay high tribute to her mother, crediting her with much of what she created. "Many of the stories that I write," she said,

"that we all write, are our mothers' stories . . . I have absorbed not only the stories themselves, but something of the manner in which she spoke of the urgency that involves the knowledge of her stories."

When Alice Walker was eight years old, she was involved in an unfortunate accident. Her younger brother accidentally shot her with a BB gun, which resulted in her losing one of her eyes. Being different from other children made her uncomfortable around most people and caused her to turn inward. It also sensitized her to the suffering of others—as sometimes occurs with individuals who are physically challenged or victimized in some manner during childhood.

Walker's isolation also made her a keen observer and lover of nature. The South of Walker's youth had no fancy malls. She grew up where there were wide-open spaces and where even the poorest of people could find quiet places of beauty to reflect in every season. In her solitude, Walker invariably studied. She became a high achiever in school. She was elected prom queen and valedictorian of her class. The problem with her eye did not prevent her from being popular among her peers, because this was a time and place where students respected good, smart individuals at the top of their class. Black teachers stressed measuring the total person.

In 1961, Alice, the neighborhood "star," went off to Spelman, the prestigious black women's college in Atlanta, Georgia, with scholarship assistance from church and community members. While studying at Spelman, Alice Walker became involved in the civil rights movement, joining ranks with other college students of her generation. In 1962, she served as a student delegate to the World Youth Peace Festival in Helsinki, Finland, and remained in Europe for the summer.

Walker transferred to Sarah Lawrence College in New York in 1963, where she began writing her first book, *Once,* a collection of poetry that was published in 1968. It was followed by *The Third Life of Grange Copeland* (1970); *The Life of Thomas Lodge* (1974); *Langston*

Hughes, American Poet (1974); *Meridian* (1976); *Good Night, Willie Lee, I'll See You in the Morning* (1979); *I Love Myself When I Am Laughing . . . and Then Again When I Am Looking Mean and Impressive: A Zora Neale Hurston Reader* (1979, editor); *You Can't Keep a Good Woman Down* (1981); *The Color Purple* (1982); *In Search of Our Mothers' Gardens and Other Essays* (1983); *Living by the Word* (1988); *The Temple of My Familiar* (1989); *Possessing the Secret Of Joy* (1992); *The Same River Twice* (1996); and her collected poems from 1965 to 1990, *Her Blue Body, Everything We Know: Earthling Poems* (1991).

An outspoken advocate for social and political change, Alice Walker consistently speaks out when she sees injustice. She was part of a civil rights protest at the White House at age eighteen. She also worked with the Legal Defense Fund in Mississippi and was a voter registration volunteer in Georgia. She traveled to Cuba to help distribute medical supplies. She helped produce a film in northern Ghana that speaks out against female circumcision, a painful ritual practiced on girls in many parts of the world. Alice Walker single-handedly resurrected the writings of Zora Neale Hurston and is credited with developing the first African American course of study in academia on the writings of black women.

The author's lifelong commitment has been against injustices to all humankind as well as nature, but her primary goal has been to uplift women. Having witnessed so much suffering among women as she grew up, her writings constantly reflect their struggle. She recalls, in an essay, a most painful scene she witnessed at age thirteen:

> . . . There she was, hardworking, large, overweight. Black, somebody's cook, lying on the slab with half her head shot off, and on her feet were the shoes . . . with a hole in the bottom [referring to a female character in her book *The Third Life of Grange Copeland*], and she had stuffed paper in them. . . . We used to have . . . just such murders as these and it was always the wife . . .

And as if knowing about the suffering of neighborhood women was not enough, Walker learned that her own grandmother had been murdered in rage by a man who claimed to have loved her. "How can a family, a community, a race, a nation, a world be healthy and strong if one half dominates the other half through threats, intimidation, and actual acts of violence?" Walker has asked.

The author is probably best known for her novel *The Color Purple*, the story of an oppressed woman, which was produced as a movie by filmmaker Steven Spielberg. Though publication of the novel met a storm of criticism from some corners of the black community, it did not destroy the book's popularity. Not only did it reach number one on the *New York Times* best-seller list, it also has the distinction of being the first novel by an African American woman to win the Pulitzer Prize in fiction. *The Color Purple* also won the National Book Award and the American Book Award.

Criticism directed at Alice Walker for the novel focused once again on the negative roles of black male characters. The author formally responded to the criticism in her book *The Same River Twice*. These same charges were launched at the artist with publication of her very first novel, *The Third Life of Grange Copeland*, which tells the story of three generations of sharecroppers. Critics who attacked the book pointed to Bronfield, a very brutal figure, to make their charge. They entirely ignored the positive qualities present in the contrasting male figure in the story.

In a conversation with Claudia Tate that appeared in *Black Women Writers at Work*, Walker explained, "I had a lot of criticism about Bronfield and my response is that I know many Bronfields, and it's a shame that I know so many. I will not ignore people like Bronfield . . ."

In addition to a career as a writer, Alice Walker has taught and lectured at colleges and universities around the country, including Jackson State, Tougaloo College, Wellesley College, the University of Massachusetts, the University of California at Berkeley, and Brandeis

Seeing with the Eye of Judgment

"You see what the behavior looks like on stage and recognize it . . . You've seen it in the real world and can judge the consequence of it. There was a time when behavior was judged much more strictly than it is now. If [a young black female] was walking down the street and some black man felt he was perfectly right to accost her and say sneaky, nasty little things to her, the community would have risen up and said, 'That's wrong! This is Miss So-and-So's child.' There was a time when the community looked at this kind of behavior with the eye of judgment."

—Alice Walker

University. She has been an editor for *Ms.* magazine and written for numerous publications. Her awards and special recognition, besides the prestigious Pulitzer Prize in 1983, are a Breadloaf Fellowship (1966), a National Endowment for the Arts grant (1969), a Radcliffe Institute Fellowship (1971), the Lillian Smith Award for poetry (1973), the National Book Award nomination for poetry (1973), the Richard and Hinda Rosenthal Foundation Award from the American Academy and Institute of Arts and Letters (1974), a Guggenheim Fellowship (1983), a MacDowell Colony Fellowship (1977), and the American Book Award and the National Book Award (1983).

Walker, who describes herself as a womanist writer, currently lives in California. She was married and divorced from civil rights attorney Melvyn Rosenman Leventhal, with whom she has a daughter, Rebecca. A graduate of Yale, Rebecca also writes.

OCTAVIA
BUTLER

(B. 1947)

✦

Octavia Butler, a leader in the genre of science fiction writing, says that she "did not decide to become a science fiction author, it just happened." A writer since she was ten years old, Butler recalls the exact moment when she decided she could write science fiction: Watching a poorly scripted science fiction movie on television at age twelve, she turned it off, convinced that she could do better. She has been writing science fiction ever since.

✦Science fiction is a **genre**, or type of fiction. Some other genres are horror and romance fiction.

Born in Pasadena, California, Butler did not know her father, who died shortly after her birth. She was raised by her mother and grandmother in a strict Baptist household. Her "church girl" upbringing gave Butler a lot of time at home, which she spent reading. As a teenager, she read science fiction magazines such as *Amazing*, *Fantasy and Science Fiction*, and *Galaxy*. As she grew older, Butler graduated to the classics of science fiction, reading such authors as Ursula Le

edwidge danticat trey ellis omar tyree **valerie wilson wesley**

premier issue

black issues

BOOK REVIEW

$4.95

January-February 1999
display until February 27

THE GOOD MARSHALL
*A Conversation
with Biographer
Juan Williams*

LIFE-TIME LOVERS
**Ossie & Ruby
The Haizlips**

OCTAVIA BUTLER
**Best-selling
Futuristic Storyteller**
Plus:
Walter Mosley joins her posse
Mind-Tripping through the 21st Century

Guin, author of *Dispossessed*, and Frank Herbert, author of the *Dune* series.

Upon graduating from high school, she attended Pasadena City College, State University in Los Angeles, and the Clarion Science Fiction Writers Workshop. Butler was discovered by the author Harlan Ellison through a Writers Guild "Open Door" program. She began work on her *Patternist* series soon after. The *Patternist* series includes *Patternmaster* (1976), *Mind of My Mind* (1977), *Survivor* (1978), *Wild Seed* (1980), and *Clay's Art* (1984). Other works by Butler are *Kindred* (1988), her best-known book, and *Parable of the Sower* (1993), her most recent. Butler also writes short stories, many of which are collected in *Bloodchild and Other Stories* (1995).

Through the use of black characters, Butler brings politics to the genre of science fiction. Her popular novel *Kindred* casts a black woman, who is married to a white man and living in suburban Los Angeles in the 1970s, back into the time of slavery. A product of the 1960s generation, Butler is convinced that the hardships and oppressions endured by her mother, grandmother, and others who came before would probably have killed most of the young folks who judged them harshly. *Kindred* illustrates both the suffering endured and the price paid by previous generations.

The author explains why: "I was involved with some people who went off on the deep end with the generation gap. They would say things like, I would like to get rid of that older generation that betrayed us . . . They didn't know what they were talking about . . . They did not know what [these elders] had gone through and what it had cost them . . . " Wise elder characters are woven into the stories she tells. It becomes a way of paying homage to their commitment and struggle.

Though more black women are now beginning to produce science fiction, the numbers remain small compared to other genres. Butler believes that the reason there are so few women who write in this

genre is that for many years, science fiction was looked upon as a medium exclusively for boys, especially "nerdy" boys. She also believes that the movies helped create and maintain this perception with their juvenile and caricature-type screen portrayal of science fiction stories. Gradually, however, the genre matured. Science fiction lovers like Butler grew up and began to write better and more mature material.

The author's first stories were published at age twenty-three, and since the publication of her first novel in 1975, she has written and published continually. At age twenty-seven, Butler had found herself laid off from her steady job and dependent on unemployment and her writing for support. She wrote feverishly and desperately, saying that there were times when she worried that her efforts at being a successful writer would be unrealized, and that maybe she should follow the advice of relatives and seek out the security of a civil service job. She recalls at the time, "I was really grabbing at straws, I don't think that I could have quit writing, but it would have been very bad for me if I had gone on and written those three novels [to no avail]."

Fortunately for Octavia Butler, and for American literature, she succeeded. A large and diverse audience reads her books today. A Hugo (1984) and Nebula award-winner, she was among a group of special honorees at the 1997 International Women Writers Conference held at New York University. When presented with the award, Octavia Butler was described as an inspiration to young African Americans who are considering creating in this field.

NTOZAKE
SHANGE

(B. 1948)

◆

Almost twenty years had passed since Lorraine Hansberry's *A Raisin in the Sun* before there was another Broadway production by a black woman. With the production of *For Colored Girls Who Have Considered Suicide When the Rainbow Is Enuf*, Ntozake Shange became the second woman to achieve this distinction.

Born Paulette Williams in Trenton, New Jersey, on October 18, the artist, like many of her peers, changed her name to protest her Westernized name, the "slave name" she inherited and the oppression it signified. Ntozake Shange's new name came from the Zulu language and means "she who comes with her own things; and she who walks like a lion."

Like Hansberry, Shange came from an upper-class family. Her father, Paul T. Williams, was a surgeon; and her mother, Eloise Williams, a psychiatric social worker and educator. They moved to St. Louis, Missouri, when Shange was eight, and bused her to a formerly segregated German American school. Like many proud African American parents, the Williamses felt that being part of the early

experiment to integrate schools was a good and noble thing. Ntozake Shange would later fictionalize the harsh experience in her novel *Betsy Brown* (1985).

The Williams family returned to Trenton when Shange was sixteen. The isolation she had experienced as a part of the desegregation experiment made her introspective and an avid reader. Some of the authors she read as a teenager were Dostoyevsky, Melville, Carson McCullers, Edna St. Vincent Millay, and Simone de Beauvoir. This was the basis of her earliest interest in the exploration of ideas. With parents who were both socially and politically active, she was exposed to prominent people, such as entertainers Josephine Baker, Chuck Berry, Charlie Parker, and Miles Davis. The scholar-activist W. E. B. Du Bois was also a frequent visitor in her parents' home.

Shange earned a B.A. from Barnard College in New York in 1970, and an M.A. in English literature from Berkeley the following year. She was married and divorced from a law student, and she taught women's and African American studies from 1972 to 1975 at various institutions in California. While living on the West Coast, she formed friendships with artists who shared her interests and politics. Shange began reciting poetry and performing with dance groups, and it was in this setting that she developed her play *Colored Girls*.

Produced in 1976 by Joseph Papp at the Public Theater in New York City, Shange's play, or *choreopoem* (poems performed with dance and music), had an enthusiastic reception. It won an Obie (off-Broadway) award, which led to the play's Broadway production. Shange received national and international acclaim.

The staging of the production featured seven women dressed in rainbow colors, reciting the day-to-day struggles of the black woman in fourteen poems. Through words, drama, and dance, the women addressed issues of self-esteem, relationships with men, and female friendships and support. *Colored Girls* was largely applauded by contemporary black women, who up until this point had never had a

Ntozake Shange's For Colored Girls Who Have Considered Suicide When the Rainbow Is Enuf *jacket cover features a beautiful drawing of the playwright.*

public forum to express so many of their thoughts and emotions. Throughout the choreopoem, there are instances when the women speak of love and the need to be in partnership with black men; but once again, critics focused only on the negative male character of "Beau Willie," a spouse abuser. Ntozake explained to her critics that she wrote the character based on having overheard a man physically abuse a woman. As the man beat the woman unmercifully, he laughed out at her screams of agony. Hearing this and recalling that she herself experienced the same torment, Ntozake says she decided to write about it.

For critics touting the time-worn adage that "the black community shouldn't air their dirty laundry," Shange has declared, "I will not be part of this conspiracy of silence. I will not do it. . . . It is my responsibility to break this silence. So that is why I wrote about Beau Willie Brown. I'm tired of living lies." The author made these comments in *Black Women Writers at Work*. Explaining further about why she wrote *Colored Girls*, Shange says that she wanted to give younger women information that she did not have.

Other notable Shange plays are *Boogie Woogie Landscapes* (1978) and *Spell #7* (1979). Besides plays, Shange has written collections of poetry, prose, and fiction. Her poetry and prose include *Natural Disasters and Other Festive Occasions* (1977), *See No Evil: Prefaces, Essays,*

BREAKING THE SILENCE

Here is what Ntozake has to say: "To break the silence is my responsibility and I'm absolutely committed to it. When I die, I will not be guilty of having left a generation of girls behind thinking that anyone can tend to their emotional health other than themselves . . ."

Accounts 1976–83 (1984), *Ridin' the Moon in Texas: Word Paintings* (1987), and *If God Can Cook So Can I* (1998). Her novels are *Sassafrass, Cypress & Indigo* (1982) and *Betsy Brown* (1985).

The literary assaults to which Ntozake Shange was subjected were probably the most mean-spirited since those launched against Zora Neale Hurston. Sadly, she would not be the last to feel the heat as more women dared speak up and tell their stories. Ntozake Shange survived the criticism and jealousy that came with her success. If there are emotional scars, the artist wears them well, and she continues to write and perform with great style.

Terry
McMILLAN
(B. 1951)

✦

Born on October 18, 1951, in Port Huron, Michigan, Terry McMillan was the eldest of Madeline Washington Tilman and Edward McMillan's five children. Terry was very close to her mother, who worked at various jobs and taught her children to be strong individuals.

Life was not easy for the McMillan family. Terry's parents struggled with many personal difficulties and eventually divorced when she was thirteen. When Terry's father died three years later, she took a job shelving books at the Port Huron library to help her mother make ends meet.

Suddenly Terry discovered the world of books. When she found a book by James Baldwin, she was surprised, because until then she had not realized that there were any African American writers. She was inspired. Just a few years later, Terry would major in journalism at the University of California at Berkeley and publish her first short story.

After her graduation from Berkeley in 1979, McMillan moved to New York City, where her life soon changed in several ways. She

PHOTO BY JONATHAN EXLEY

began studies that eventually led to a graduate degree in film from the School of Journalism at Columbia University. A single mother, she had a son whom she named Solomon. And she joined the Harlem Writers Guild.

In the early 1980s, Terry McMillan brought new energy and a bold voice to the Harlem Writers Guild. Reading from her work-in-progress, *Mama* (1987), the newcomer was anything but the shy person that most first-time readers were when presenting to the group. It was clear that Terry knew that she was good and did not need that kind of assurance from others. McMillan completed her story, her way, and has since published not only *Mama* but *Disappearing Acts* (1989), *Breaking Ice: An Anthology of Contemporary African American Fiction* (1989), *Waiting to Exhale* (1982), and *How Stella Got Her Groove Back* (1996). The last two books have been adapted for screenplays, with McMillan writing the scripts herself to ensure that the film tells the story she narrates in the book.

Hardworking and determined, McMillan developed clear goals. Not only did she produce her first book while working full-time, but she planned a one-woman publicity campaign that got her books in stores, colleges, and universities across the country. An attractive, smart, and articulate young woman, McMillan understood the need for marketing her books. She knew that many good books have died quietly because of a lack of know-how by publishers to market a particular title.

✦Advertisements are one way books are **marketed** so that people will want to buy them.

The author has shared stories of rising before daylight to write before going to work. It is a story that many contemporary writers tell when revealing what they went through to become successful. The sacrifice and hard work have more than paid off for Terry McMillan. All of her titles have sold well, and her audience eagerly awaits her next new book.

The author has been interviewed on numerous television shows. Terry McMillan has proven to the publishing industry that there is, indeed, a readership for stories by and about the lives of black women. Successful books by Bebe Moore Campbell, Valerie Wesley Wilson, and other best-selling black women writers have confirmed it. Today, whenever there is a discussion about African American literature, Terry McMillan's name is sure to be mentioned.

THE NEXT GENERATION

Rosemary Bray, like McMillan, was a young member of the Harlem Writers Guild. Bray, like many early black women, has written her memoir. Her parents were poor southerners who had migrated to Chicago from Mississippi. Bray, born in 1955, shares the story of her family's struggle in a moving memoir titled *Unafraid of the Dark* (1998). A graduate of Yale University, Bray has served as editor and written for numerous national magazines and newspapers, including *Ms.*, *Essence*, the *Daily News*, and the *New York Times*.

OTHER NOTED WRITERS

I wish I had the space to name every accomplished black woman writer! There were many early American writers such as **Nelle Larsen, Anna J. Cooper, Georgia Douglas Johnson,** and important figures of the first generation of the Harlem Writers Guild such as **Rosa Guy, Louise Merriweather, Alice Childress,** and **Sarah E. Wright.**

Many more writers emerged after the 1950s, including **Sonia Sanchez, June Jordan, Mari Evans, Jayne Cortez, Alexis Deveaux, Carolyn Rodgers, Sherley A. Williams, Ellease Southerland, Gloria Naylor, Gayl Jones, Rita Dove, Connie Porter, Marita Golden, bell hooks, Thulani Davis,** and **Grace Edwards;** the young new visionary poet **jessica care moore;** religion authors **Delores Williams, Katie Cannon, Renita Weems,** and **Suzanne J. Cook;** writers of meditation and reflection, such as **Iyanla Vanzant, Marian Wright Edelman,** and **Susan Taylor.** There are the scholarly authors, such as professors **Angela Davis, Lani Guinier,** and **Patricia Williams;** award-winning novelists **A. J. Verdelle** and **Edwidge Danticat;** best-selling novelists **Connie Briscoe** and **J. California Cooper;** folk and culinary writer **Verta Mae Grosvenor;** and social critic **Michelle Wallace.** There are the acclaimed novelists **Michelle Cliff, Eleanor Taylor Bland, Lorene Cary, Kristin Hunter, Benilde Little,** and **Sapphire;** playwrights **Adrienne Kennedy, Micki Grant, Shaunueille Perry, J. E. Franklin,** and hundreds of prominent and ordinary black women who have written autobiographies that inform and inspire.

In my list, I would also include journalists such as **Charlayne Hunter-Gault, Marcia Gillespie, Audrey Edwards, Jill Nelson, Lisa Jones, Isabel Wilkerson, Margo Jefferson, E. R. Shipp, Ida Lewis,** and **Cynthia Tucker.**

Recommended Reading for Children and Young Adults

A seldom-heralded group of black women writers create especially for children and teens. Several of these writers have won important honors; all of them deserve praise for enriching our lives. Here are a few of the leaders and some of their best books for young people. You can read more about these books and authors in *Black Books Galore! Guide to Great African American Children's Books* (John Wiley & Sons, 1998).

Tanya Bolden

Through Loona's Door: A Tammy and Owen Adventure with Carter G. Woodson. (1997). Ages 9–11. A brother and sister go back in time and learn about black history.

Just Family (1996). Ages 12 and up. A girl discovers a secret about her family.

Lucille Clifton

The Lucky Stone (1979). Ages 9–11. A young girl inherits an ancient, enchanted good-luck piece.

Eloise Greenfield

Talk about a Family (1978). Ages 9–11. A girl's father and mother are not getting along and her life is about to change.

Sister (1974). Ages 12 and up. A teenager rereads the diary she has kept since she was a little girl.

Nikki Grimes

From a Child's Heart (1993). Ages 9–11. The author shares children's prayers and poems.

Meet Danitra Brown (1994). Ages 9–11. Two best friends express their friendship in poems.

ROSA GUY

The Friends (1973). Ages 12 and up. Two teenagers discover how much they need each other.

VIRGINIA HAMILTON

Cousins (1990). Ages 9–11. A young girl learns to cope with difficult but common family problems.

Sweet Whispers, Brother Rush (1982). Ages 12 and up. A stranger comes into a teenager's life and turns it upside down by taking her back to her childhood.

JOYCE HANSEN

Which Way Freedom? (1986). Ages 12 and up. A teenage runaway slave joins the Union Army during the Civil War.

Yellow Bird and Me (1986). Ages 12 and up. A New York City girl makes a friend who is having trouble in school.

SHARON BELL MATHIS

The Hundred Penny Box (1975). Ages 9–11. A boy protects his great-great aunt.

Red Dog, Blue Fly: Football Poems (1991). Ages 9–11. Football lovers get a whole book of poems about their sport.

PATRICIA C. MCKISSACK

The Dark-Thirty: Southern Tales of the Supernatural (1992). Ages 12 and up. The author tells scary stories with roots in African American history.

A Picture of Freedom: The Diary of Clotee, A Slave Girl, Belmont Plantation, Virginia 1859 (1997). Ages 12 and up. A slave girl who learns to read in secret keeps a diary.

ANNE MOODY

Coming of Age in Mississippi (1968). Ages 12 and up. The author's true story of growing up during the height of the civil rights era.

EMILY MOORE

Just My Luck (1982). Ages 9–11. A lonely girl and her creepy neighbor have an adventure finding a missing dog.

Something to Count On (1980). Ages 9–11. A young girl has to decide what to do about her unpredictable father.

MILDRED TAYLOR

Roll of Thunder, Hear My Cry (1976). Ages 12 and up. A proud family stands up for their rights in the rural South during the Great Depression in this much-honored classic.

MILDREN PITTS WALTER

Mississippi Challenge (1992). Ages 12 and up. Dramatic events of the civil rights era unfold through the eyes of the actual participants.

Second Daughter: The Story of a Slave Girl (1996). Ages 12 and up. Two sisters who are slaves during the American Revolution decide to sue their master for their freedom.

JACQUELINE WOODSON

I Hadn't Meant to Tell You This (1994). Ages 12 and up. A popular girl makes an unpopular friend who asks her to keep a terrible secret.

Last Summer with Maizon (1992). Ages 12 and up. Two best friends face being separated from each other.

Take time to read as many of these works as you can. You will be grateful.

CHRONOLOGY

1753? Phillis Wheatley born

1761 Phillis Wheatley arrives in Boston aboard slave ship

1767 Phillis Wheatley writes first work, *A Poem by Phillis, a Negro Girl, on the Death of Reverend George Whitefield* (published 1770)

1773 Phillis Wheatley's *Poems on Various Subjects, Religious and Moral*, becomes first book written by a black in North America and second by a woman

1775 Revolutionary War begins

1776 George Washington receives Phillis Wheatley at his Cambridge, Massachusetts, headquarters after receiving poem she writes in praise of him

1783 Revolutionary War ends

1784 Phillis Wheatley dies

1797 Sojourner (Isabella Hurley) Truth born

1812 War of 1812

1813 Harriet Jacobs born

1825 Frances E. W. Harper born

1827 Slavery abolished in New York

1843 Sojourner Truth begins itinerant preaching

1845 Frances E. W. Harper's *Forest Leaves* (of which no copies remain) is published

1850 Sojourner Truth's *Narrative of Sojourner Truth, a Northern Slave, Emancipated from Bodily Servitude by the State of New York in 1828*, as narrated to Olive Gilbert, is published

1851 Sojourner Truth delivers "Ain't I a Woman" speech at women's rights meeting in Akron, Ohio

1852 White novelist Harriet Beecher Stowe's *Uncle Tom's Cabin*, a book on slavery, sells over 300,000 copies in the United States in its first year of publication

1859 Abolitionist John Brown leads unsuccessful raid on Harper's Ferry

1861 Civil War begins

Harriet Jacobs's *Incidents in the Life of a Slave Girl Written by Herself* (under the name of Linda Brent) is published

1862 President Abraham Lincoln issues preliminary Emancipation Proclamation

Ida B. Wells born

1863 Emancipation Proclamation frees slaves in Confederate states

1865 Civil War ends

1867 Reconstruction years begin

1875 Alice Moore Dunbar Nelson born

1877 Reconstruction years end

1883 Sojourner Truth dies

1884 Jessie Redmon Fauset born

1891 Ida B. Wells becomes part owner of a Memphis newspaper

Zora Neale Hurston born

1892 Frances E. W. Harper's novel *Iola Leroy,* the best-selling novel by an African American in the nineteenth century, is published

1895 Alice Dunbar Nelson's first book, *Violets and Other Tales*, is published

1897 Harriet Jacobs dies

1905 Jessie Redmon Fauset becomes first black woman admitted to Phi Beta Kappa.

1907 Dorothy West born

1910 Origin of NAACP (National Association for the Advancement of Colored People)

Publication of *Crisis* magazine, official news organ of the NAACP, with W. E. B. Du Bois as editor

Ida B. Wells, anti-lynching crusader, becomes president of Negro Fellowship League

1911 Frances E. W. Harper dies

Ann Petry born

1915 Margaret Walker Alexander born

1917 Gwendolyn Brooks born

United States enters World War I

1928 Maya Angelou born

1929 Onset of the Great Depression

Paule Marshall (Valenza Pauline Burke) born

1930 Lorraine Hansberry born

Zora Neale Hurston co-authors a comedy, *Mule Bone*, with the poet Langston Hughes

1931 Ida B. Wells-Barnett dies

Toni Morrison born

1934 Zora Neale Huston's first novel, *Jonah's Gourd Vine*, is published

Audre Lorde born

1935 Alice Moore Dunbar Nelson dies

1936 Lucille Clifton born

1939 Toni Cade Bambara born

1941 United States enters World War II

1942 Margaret Walker Alexander's poem "For My People" is published

1943 Nikki Giovanni born

1944   Alice Walker born

1945   Debut of John Johnson's *Ebony* magazine

Gwendolyn Brooks's first book of poetry, *A Street in Bronzeville*, is published

Ann Petry's *The Street* is published

1947   Octavia Butler born

1948   Ntozake Shange born

1949   Jamaica Kincaid born

1950   Gwendolyn Brooks, the first African American so honored, is awarded a Pulitzer Prize for her book of poetry *Annie Allen*

1951   Terry McMillan born

1953   Gwendolyn Brooks's semi-autobiographical novel, *Maude Martha*, is published

Debut of author James Baldwin's *Go Tell It on the Mountain*

1954   *Brown* v. *Board of Education of Topeka* reverses *Plessy* v. *Ferguson* by declaring segregated schools and other public facilities that are separated by race inherently unequal

Paule Marshall's first short story, "The Valley Between," is published

1955   Murder of Emmett Till, fourteen-year-old Chicago boy visiting in Mississippi

Rosemary Bray born

1959   Publication of Paule Marshall's semi-autobiographical novel, *Brown Girl, Brownstones*

Lorraine Hansberry becomes first black woman to have a play produced on Broadway

1960   Zora Neale Hurston dies

1961   Jessie Redmon Fauset dies

1964   Beginning of the Black Arts Movement

1965   Lorraine Hansberry dies

1966 Margaret Walker Alexander's *Jubilee* is published

1968 Nikki Giovanni's first volume of poetry, *Black Feelings, Black Talk*, is published

Alice Walker's first volume of poetry, *Once*, is published

Gwendolyn Brooks is named poet laureate of Illinois

1969 Lucille Clifton's first book, *Good Times*, is published

1970 Publication of *Essence*, magazine for black women

Publication of Toni Morrison's first novel, *The Bluest Eye*

Publication of Maya Angelou's *I Know Why the Caged Bird Sings*, first installment of her autobiography

Publication of *The Black Woman: An Anthology*, with Toni Cade Bambara as editor

1973 Lorraine Hansberry's play *A Raisin in the Sun* becomes a musical, *Raisin*

1976 Premier in New York of Ntozake Shange's *For Colored Girls Who Have Considered Suicide When the Rainbow Is Enuf*

1977 Toni Morrison's *Song of Solomon* becomes the second book by an African American to be selected as a Book-of-the Month Club selection

1978 Toni Morrison wins National Book Critics Circle Award for *Song of Solomon*

1979 Lucille Clifton is named poet laureate of Maryland

1981 Toni Morrison's *Tar Baby* becomes national best-seller

1983 Alice Walker is awarded Pulitzer Prize for *The Color Purple*

1984 Octavia Butler wins the Hugo Award

1985 Gwendolyn Brooks becomes the first black to be appointed poetry consultant to the Library of Congress

1987 Forty-eight black authors sign letter of protest for failure of Toni Morrison's book *Beloved* to receive the National Book Award

Toni Morrison is awarded the Pulitzer Prize for *Beloved*

1992 Audre Lorde dies

Toni Morrison has three publications: a novel, *Jazz;* a book of criticism, *Playing in the Dark;* and *Race-ing Justice, En-Gendering Power,* a book of essays on the Clarence Thomas hearings, for which she serves as editor

1993 Toni Morrison wins Nobel Prize for literature

Maya Angelou reads her poem "On the Pulse of the Morning" at the inauguration of President Bill Clinton

1995 Toni Cade Bambara dies

1997 Ann Petry dies

1998 Dorothy West dies

Margaret Walker Alexander dies

BIBLIOGRAPHY

BOOKS

Bell, Roseann P., Bettye J. Parker, Patricia Bell Scott, and Beverly Guy-Sheftal. *Sturdy Black Bridges.* New York: Doubleday, 1979.

Brooks, Gwendolyn. *The World of Gwendolyn Brooks.* New York: Harper & Row, 1971.

Busby, Margaret. *Daughters of Africa.* New York: Ballantine Books, 1992.

Evans, Mari, ed. *Black Women Writers (1950-1980): A Critical Evaluation.* New York: Anchor/Doubleday, 1984.

Foster, Frances Smith, ed. *A Brighter Coming Day: A Frances Ellen Watkins Harper Reader.* New York: Feminist Press 1980.

Franklin, John Hope, and August Meir, eds. *Black Leaders of the Twentieth Century.* Urbana: University of Illinois Press, 1982.

Gates, Henry Louis Jr., ed. *The Schomburg Library of Nineteenth-Century Black Women Writers.* Cambridge, Mass.: Oxford University Press, 1988.

Gates, Henry Louis Jr., and Nellie Y. McKay, eds. *The Norton Anthology of African American Literature.* New York: W.W. Norton & Company, 1977.

Giddings, Paula. *When and Where I Enter: The Impact of Black Women on Race and Sex in America.* New York: William Morrow & Company, 1984.

Harley, Sharon. *The Timetables of African American History: A Chronology of the Most Important People and Events in African American History.* New York: Touchstone/Simon & Schuster, 1996.

Hull, Gloria T., Patricia Bell Scott, and Barbara Smith. *But Some of Us Are Brave.* New York: Feminist Press, 1982.

Lanker, Brian, and Barbara Summers. *I Dream a World: Portraits of Black Women Who Changed America.* New York: Stewart, Tabori, Chang, 1989.

Lerner, Gerda, ed. *Black Women in White America: A Documentary History.* New York: Vintage/Random House, 1972.

Marshall, Paule. *Reena and Other Stories.* New York: Feminist Press, 1983.

Noble, Jean. *Beautiful Also Are the Souls of My Sisters: A History of the Black Woman in America.* Englewood Cliffs, N.J.: Prentice-Hall, 1978.

Pace, Donelson, and Nilsen Allen Pace. *Literature for Today's Young Adults.* Glenview, Ill.: Scott, Foresman & Company, 1980.

Rose, Lorraine Elena, and Ruth Elizabeth Randolph. *Harlem's Glory: Black Writing (1900–1950).* Cambridge, Mass.: Harvard University Press, 1996.

Sterling, Dorothy, ed. *We Are Your Sisters: Black Women in the Nineteenth Century.* New York: W.W. Norton & Company, 1913.

Tate, Claudia. *Black Women Writers at Work.* New York: Continuum, 1984.

Wade-Gayes, Gloria. *No Crystal Stair: Visions of Race and Gender in Black Women's Fiction.* Cleveland: The Pilgrim Press, 1997.

Walker, Alice. *I Love Myself When I Am Laughing: A Zora Neale Hurston Reader.* New York: Feminist Press, 1979.

Walker, Margaret. *On Being Female, Black, and Free: Essays.* Knoxville: University of Tennessee Press, 1998.

Washington, Mary Helen, ed. *Black-Eyed Susans and Midnight Birds: Stories by and about Black Women.* New York: Anchor/Doubleday, 1990 (originally published 1975 & 1980).

————, ed. *Invented Lives: Narratives of Black Women (1860-1960).* New York: Anchor/Doubleday, 1987.

AUTOBIOGRAPHIES

Angelou, Maya. *I Know Why the Caged Bird Sings*. New York: Random House, 1970.

Bray, Rosemary. *Un-Afraid of the Dark*. New York: Random House, 1988.

BIOGRAPHIES

Century, Douglas. *Toni Morrison: Black American of Achievement*. New York: Chelsea House, 1994.

Gentry, Tony. *Alice Walker: Black American of Achievement*. New York: Chelsea House 1993.

Richmond, Merele. *Phillis Wheatley: American Women of Achievement*. New York: Chelsea House, 1988.

Witcover, Paul. *Zora Neale Hurston: Black American of Achievement*. New York: Chelsea House, 1991.

ARTICLES

"Maya Angelou: Lessons in Living," by Susan Taylor, *Essence* (December 1992): 49–53.

"The Black Woman Writer and the Diaspora" ("Sisterhood and Survival," essay by Audre Lorde; and "Black Women and the Science Fiction Genre: An Interview with Octavia Butler"). *Black Scholar* (March–April 1966): 14–15.

"A Society of One: Zora Neale Hurston, American Contrarian," by Claudia Roth Pierpoint. *New Yorker* (February 1997): 80–91.

NEWSPAPERS

"Remembering Dorothy West," by Howard Kissel, in the New York *Daily News,* August 26, 1998.

Review of *Trouble in Mind*, April 23, 1998, in the New York *Amsterdam News.*

Report of 90th Birthday of Dorothy West, September 11, 1997, in the New York *Amsterdam News*.

Obituary of Ann Petry, April 30, 1997, in the *New York Times*.

Obituary of Dorothy West, by Andrew L. Yarrow, August 19, 1998, in the *New York Times*.

Obituary of Margaret Walker Alexander, December 4, 1998, in the *New York Times*.

PICTURE CREDITS

Lenox and Tilden Foundations; page 95: courtesy of the Library of Congress, Washington, D.C.; page 96: courtesy of Jewell Gresham Nemiroff; page 98: courtesy of Archive Photos; page 104: courtesy of Photographs and Print Division, Schomburg Center for Research in Black Culture, The New York Public Library/Astor, Lenox and Tilden Foundations; page 108: courtesy of BOA Editions, Ltd.; page 113: courtesy of Pantheon Books, a division of Random House, Inc.; page 118: courtesy of Photographs and Print Division, Schomburg Center for Research in Black Culture, The New York Public Library/Astor, Lenox and Tilden Foundations; page 120: courtesy of the Library of Congress, Washington, D.C.; page 123: courtesy of Capri/Saga/Archive Photos; page 129: courtesy of *Black Issues Book Review,* a Cox, Matthews & Associates, Inc., publication, Fairfax, Va.; page 133: courtesy of Photographs and Print Division, Schomburg Center for Research in Black Culture, The New York Public Library/Astor, Lenox and Tilden Foundations; page 135: courtesy of Bantam Books, a division of Random House, Inc.; page 139: courtesy of Jonathan Exley, Los Angeles.

INDEX